HARTSHORNE AND NEOCLASSICAL METAPHYSICS

HARTSHORNE

AND

NEOCLASSICAL
METAPHYSICS

An Interpretation

Eugene H. Peters

UNIVERSITY OF NEBRASKA PRESS · LINCOLN

Manufactured in the United States of America

CONTENTS

PREFACE

STYLES IN PHILOSOPHY, THOUGH SELDOM AS UNPREDICTABLE
as ladies' fashions, do not endure without change or without alternative. In the English-speaking world, philosophy since the twenties has been powerfully influenced by
nonmetaphysical (and even antimetaphysical) tendencies.
Chief among them has been analysis, whose lineage includes such notables as Bertrand Russell, G. E. Moore,
and Ludwig Wittgenstein. It may of course be argued
that in the American scene there has been a place for
all comers, regardless of creed. Still, it cannot plausibly
be claimed that in recent decades metaphysicians have
commanded the stage or even that they have enjoyed
supporting roles. There have doubtless been good reasons for indifference toward metaphysics; the excesses
and flamboyance of nineteenth-century metaphysics
called for reaction. But neglect of metaphysics has meant
that many students of philosophy have received only a
superficial introduction to the long history of speculative
philosophy and scarcely more than a glimpse at twentieth-
century developments.

The aim of this book is to present an interpretation of a metaphysician who for more than forty years has been constructing a new system of philosophy. The work of Charles Hartshorne, though widely acknowledged, is little known. Indeed, there are few volumes which undertake to treat his thought. It would be difficult to summarize the content of Hartshorne's voluminous writing. What I have done is rather to select a cluster of "fundamentals" upon which the system rests, and I have focused on these. My contention is that Hartshorne develops each of these fundamental ideas in the light of a single methodological principle, a principle which expresses his very conception of metaphysics. Accordingly, I have placed a chapter on "the methodological key" early in the book.

The closer one examines Hartshorne's treatment of such concepts as experience, creativity, and deity, the more he becomes aware of the connections between those concepts, and the greater becomes his appreciation of the unity of Hartshorne's metaphysics. What I have called the methodological key is not employed by Hartshorne in a pat, dogmatic way. But metaphysics has its ways and means, as does science or mathematics, and it must therefore have its distinctive criteria. If so, a system of metaphysics can be expected to exhibit a formal coherence insofar as it is sustained by its method. I have tried to bring into view that coherence in Hartshorne's metaphysics.

No doubt there are other ways of seeing Hartshorne,

ways which for certain purposes may be quite valuable. One could discuss Hartshorne from the point of view of his concern with down-to-earth problems such as war, population, decision making, and the sense of personal worth. Or one could study the intellectual tradition into which Hartshorne fits, explain at length the influences on his philosophical development, and trace in detail the relation of his thought to C. S. Peirce, A. N. Whitehead, and others. My aim, however, has been to see Hartshorne's metaphysics as a system and to grasp its essential structure.

Hartshorne calls his system a form of "neoclassical metaphysics." It shares much with classical forms. There is concern with the great questions, with issues of cosmic scope, and in general with the problem of reality itself. Moreover, Hartshorne is a rationalist in the sense that he takes falsity in metaphysics as a form of failure in meaning. The system is new and advances beyond classical forms of metaphysics in a number of ways. Its basic departure is that it makes becoming rather than static being the fundamental, inclusive principle of all things. In addition, Hartshorne places far greater value on concrete feeling and experience than did the classical tradition and gives the categories of aesthetics a prominence in the interpretation of reality. Hence, the rationalism of his process metaphysics is not at odds with the concrete features of the world but preserves the essential concerns of existentialist philosophers.

If sympathetic appreciation is helpful in the understanding of a philosopher, I can claim that advantage. Yet I have at the same time tried to maintain a distance from Hartshorne, not only because each philosopher has a responsibility to do his own thinking but also because as interpreter and expositor I have required an angle of perspective on him. And at the end of the book I have raised a few questions in a critical vein, since every philosophy deserves the help of critical interrogation, and Hartshorne, as he says, has received far too little critical attention.

A generous research grant from Hiram College made it possible for me to be in continuous touch with Charles and Dorothy Hartshorne during the months this manuscript was in preparation. They were most hospitable, and I enjoyed hours of conversation with them. Professor Hartshorne read each chapter on its completion and made many helpful suggestions. I am indebted to Dorothy Hartshorne for much of the biographical detail included in chapter one. I have been privileged to have Professor Irwin C. Lieb of the University of Texas as a reader of the manuscript; for his interest and comments I am grateful. To my wife Damaris I wish to express gratitude, not only for typing the entire manuscript, but for her encouragement during the writing of these pages and for her patience.

»»»»»»»»»»»»»»»»»»»»»»»» HARTSHORNE
AND NEOCLASSICAL
METAPHYSICS

CHARLES HARTSHORNE

«««««««««««««««««««««««

CHARLES HARTSHORNE WAS BORN IN KITTANNING, PENN-
sylvania, on June 5, 1897. His father, a man of English
descent, was then the rector at the Episcopal church of
Kittanning. For generations Hartshornes had been
Quakers, but Hartshorne's grandfather had "married
out of meeting" and was obliged to leave the Society of
Friends. He became an Episcopalian, and his son Francis
Cope Hartshorne, though trained in law, became a
clergyman of the church. The grandfather was a man of
some wealth, having served as vice-president of the
Lehigh Valley Railroad. For him Charles Hartshorne
was named. Hartshorne was the second of six children,
of whom only one, the oldest, was a girl.

Charles and his brother Richard attended Yeates
School, an Episcopal boarding school located in the
country, five miles from Lancaster, Pennsylvania. In this
picturesque setting, young Hartshorne began to mature
intellectually. Here for the first time he was exposed to
the theory of evolution. His interest in the natural world

was broadened by his own investigations. Equipped with a small book by Chester Reed, *Land Birds East of the Rockies*, and a five-dollar pair of field glasses, he made a study of birds and bird song. Students at Yeates were permitted an hour and a quarter each morning after breakfast for study as they wished. Hartshorne used this time, particularly in the spring, to observe birds. Throughout his life he has continued his bird study.

Even before he entered Yeates School, Hartshorne had shown himself to be a reflective lad. His mother observed that from the age of five Charles had tended to think things out for himself. He was first stimulated to serious thought by his father's sermons. Included in his childhood reading were works of Alcott, Dickens, Hawthorne, and Kipling. By the time he was fifteen, Hartshorne was dipping into Emerson. He was able to read with unusual concentration. On one occasion, his family returned home from church to find him sitting on his bed lost in a book. "I'm all ready to go," he said. "Is it time?"

Hartshorne's father had attended General Theological Seminary in New York City and there received a good background in biblical studies. He was orthodox on basic theological points but by no means old-fashioned in outlook or interpretation. Though serious-minded and not especially outgoing, Francis Hartshorne was a kind and talented man. He had a mechanical bent, enjoyed working with his hands, and was even something of an inventor. He owned a wide assortment of tools and was one of the first in Pennsylvania to have a car—which he himself repaired when the need arose. His wife, Marguerite Haughton, was the daughter of an Episcopal clergyman. She graced the Hartshorne home with a saintly presence and outdid her husband in wit and charm. She had a gift for understanding people and met them easily.

At eighteen young Hartshorne entered Haverford College, but his career there was interrupted by the Great War. Without completing his sophomore year, he went to France to be an orderly in a base hospital on the Normandy coast. His father was critical of Haverford's pacifist dissociation from the war. He felt that instead of withdrawal, positive moral action was called for. Rufus Jones, who had been one of Hartshorne's teachers at Haverford, felt much the same way and became a moving spirit in the founding of the American Friends Service Committee. Hartshorne himself shared the idealism that had swept the nation, believing that the war was being fought to make the world safe for democracy. Yet his experience in France deeply depressed and shocked him. Though he was not involved in the fighting, he was exposed daily to the spectacle of suffering and death, and at one point the battle surged so close that it became necessary to evacuate the hospital.

Hartshorne had with him in France an extra footlocker, in which he kept some forty small volumes, many from the Everyman's Library. Reading broke the tedium of long hours of work—which often involved nothing more glorious than mopping floors. One of Hartshorne's fellow workers once undertook to explain to him the finer points of mopping. So enthusiastic a learner was Hartshorne that the man proceeded to mop the entire floor before the admiring eyes of his protégé. Apparently Hartshorne had included *Tom Sawyer* in his reading!

He had decided while at Haverford to go to Harvard to continue his education, and on returning from the war he carried out his plan. He realized early that he was not cut out for the ministry and as a boy had even prayed that he would not be led in that direction. He had from his youth shown signs of interest in philosophy. During his last year at Yeates School he had read Matthew Arnold's *Literature and Dogma* and had been shocked by Arnold's critique of Christianity. (Three aphorisms from that work have stuck with him ever since: that religion is "morality touched by emotion," that in Western theology God has been construed as "a magnified and non-natural man," and that for the Hebrews God was "the enduring power, not ourselves, which makes for righteousness.") At Haverford he had turned decisively toward philosophy. His philosophy teacher there had been Rufus Jones, a mystic and historian of mysticism, who had been influenced by the idealist J. E. Creighton of Cornell. Jones was undogmatic, did not insist on sharply defined beliefs, and taught philosophy in a common-sense way. Under him, Hartshorne, a sophomore of twenty, had read Josiah Royce, the first professional philosopher he had attempted. Jones sometimes warned his students: "Every system has an impasse somewhere." These were helpful words of caution for Hartshorne, who was soon to be engaged in system building. At the fifteenth reunion of Hartshorne's Haverford class (in 1934) Jones proudly acknowledged that Hartshorne was the first of his students to become a professional philosopher.

In the summer of 1919, having returned to the United States, Hartshorne made a trip to California, where in Berkeley he heard C. I. Lewis lecture on German idealism at the University of California. Hartshorne entered Harvard in the fall and after two years received his B.A. (1921). His undergraduate advisor was the Sanskrit scholar James Haughton Woods. The bulk of Hartshorne's course work during his two undergraduate years at Harvard was in philosophy. He also took biology and several courses in English. (At one point he had considered English as a career.) W. E. Hocking, who had been Royce's outstanding student, was an inspiration to Harvard undergraduates, and Hartshorne took his course in metaphysics. From C. I. Lewis, recently come to Harvard, he took advanced logic, and from Henry M. Sheffer, symbolic logic. He also took Sheffer's course on British empiricism. Hartshorne was in an ethics seminar under Ralph Barton Perry, who had been a favorite student of William James and was then one of the six New Realists. For a year Raphael Demos was Hartshorne's tutor. A member of Phi Beta Kappa, Hartshorne continued at Harvard after receiving his B.A. and completed an M.A. in philosophy in 1922. Taking Woods's advice, he proceeded immediately for a Ph.D. in philosophy. His graduate work included courses in psychology, which at the time was still linked departmentally with philosophy. By concentrated effort Hartshorne completed his dissertation, "The Unity of Being," in record time and was awarded the Ph.D. in June, 1923.

Hartshorne was president of the Harvard Philosophy Club one year. He was also involved in the Liberal Club, which he helped found. In order to get the club started, he and some fellow students went to President Charles W. Eliot, then in retirement, to request support, and it was granted. Among the speakers whom Hartshorne heard at the Liberal Club were Norman Angell, Upton Sinclair, Norman Hapgood, Scott Nearing, Samuel Gompers, and Red Doran.

During the eight years since he entered Haverford in 1915, Hartshorne's philosophical convictions had taken shape. His ideas differed considerably from those of other students. While at Haverford he flirted briefly with determinism. But he was never attracted to the idea of substance and was a panpsychist from the age of twenty (when the only professional philosopher he had read was Royce). Though a theist, he had little interest in becoming an apologist for Christianity. No doubt he was influenced in this regard by his reading of Emerson, Arnold, and Royce, none of whom were orthodox Christians, and also by the skeptical mood that prevailed among Haverford students. At Harvard, Hocking disabused the young philosopher of the notion that God knows all future events. Hartshorne has never abandoned the basic philosophical tenets he held at Harvard, though he has subsequently made them more definite and clear. Indeed, throughout his career Hartshorne has maintained a single system of thought, modifying it only in detail or emphasis. Perhaps the most significant exception is his forsaking the idea that an event can influence one of its contemporaries. He held this idea until the fifties, when he embraced A. N. Whitehead's doctrine of the mutual independence of contemporary events.

Hartshorne's philosophical acumen scarcely escaped notice at Harvard. Some years later (in 1933), when Lewis came to the University of Chicago to lecture, he remarked at a party that Hartshorne had been the most brilliant philosophy student Harvard had had in fifty years. On being told of Hartshorne's high estimate of the Kant course Lewis taught, Lewis replied that the course was nothing special, that instead it was what Hartshorne had made of it. There is nothing surprising in the fact that Hartshorne was awarded a Sheldon Traveling Fellowship for the year 1923/24. He decided to spend that year at the University of Freiburg and left for Germany in the summer of 1923. Arriving there, he found that the universities were observing an international summer school in Vienna. He struck out for Vienna on a bicycle, but a spill caused him to complete the trip by train. In Vienna he met Heinrich Gomperz (son of the famous historian of philosophy, Theodor Gomperz), who opened his father's immense library to Hartshorne. The American visitor took advantage of the opportunity, read a great deal while he was in Vienna, and at the same time polished up his German.

Returning to Freiburg, Hartshorne heard Edmund Husserl and Martin Heidegger, as well as the Kant scholar Julius Ebbinghaus and the Hegelian Richard Kroner. In addition, the Sheldon fellow continued to read widely. On one occasion, he and a Russian émigré tackled Dante's *Divine Comedy*. Using an Italian text and an Italian-French dictionary, the pair proceeded, discussing in French and German. Needless to say, the experiment did not take them far into Dante.

Given a second award, Hartshorne remained in Germany during the year 1924/25. When Heidegger left Freiburg to go to Marburg, Hartshorne also went there, hoping to get a better understanding of Heidegger's thought. He remained in Marburg the rest of the year. In the fall of 1925, Hartshorne was back at Harvard, this time as a research assistant. His assignment was to work on the papers of C. S. Peirce. In addition, for a semester he was assistant to Whitehead, who had come to Harvard in 1924. Hartshorne also did some teaching and was appointed an instructor.

Peirce had died in 1914 without having organized his many writings, and subsequent efforts at editing had been abortive. From 1925 to 1928 Hartshorne worked steadily on the Peirce papers. He began the project alone, working in the Peirce Room of Harvard's Widener

Library, where he found the papers in stacks on a table. In 1927 Paul Weiss, then a graduate student, became an assistant to Hartshorne and later a partner in the editorship. Weiss explained that his teacher Morris Cohen had impressed upon him the importance of Peirce. Hartshorne and Weiss worked together in selecting the materials and organizing them in accordance with a scheme Hartshorne had devised. The first volume was published in 1931 and the final (sixth) volume in 1935. Most of the work had been completed when Hartshorne left Harvard in 1928 to join the philosophy faculty of the University of Chicago.

Hartshorne's thinking was influenced by Whitehead as well as by Peirce. "I am becoming a Whiteheadian without ceasing to be a Peircian," Hartshorne once told the British metaphysician. Hartshorne and Whitehead were in fact very close in philosophical outlook, many of Whitehead's ideas being similar to ideas Hartshorne had developed in his dissertation. Hartshorne preferred Peirce's view of possibility to Whitehead's, but he accepted Whitehead rather than Peirce on actuality. Both Peirce and Whitehead reinforced in Hartshorne the conviction that aesthetic categories are fundamental. "Kant," said Whitehead, "should have written his three critiques in reverse order." Peirce, who put aesthetics ahead of ethics and logic, would have agreed.

The Whiteheads were fond of Hartshorne. One summer they invited him to visit them in New Hampshire, and he went up for several weeks. Hartshorne never permitted his studies to make him unsociable and he had many friends. As a youth he had enjoyed quite an active social life, though at Haverford he saw few girls. To a dance in Cambridge in the spring of 1926, he brought as his date Dorothy Eleanore Cooper of Chicago and Wellesley College. And the dance was a Harvard-Radcliffe affair! The Whiteheads were chaperons on that occasion, and Mrs. Hartshorne still recalls the piercing glance of Mrs. Whitehead when Hartshorne introduced her as his date.

During his first quarter of teaching at Chicago, Hartshorne lived in the Disciples Divinity House. Miss Cooper was at that time back in Chicago studying music and editing for a publishing house. Hartshorne would visit her, occasionally bringing with him a handful of manuscripts from the Peirce project. At the end of the quarter, on December 22, 1928, they were married. Their only child, Emily Lawrence, was born in 1940.

Hartshorne, at thirty-three, was invited to deliver a paper at the International Congress of Philosophy held at Oxford in 1930. He accepted and made the trip, accompanied by Mrs. Hartshorne. Whitehead, who also attended, told her while there that he felt it important for the remaining work on the Peirce volumes, already at the Harvard Press, to be completed. Following the Congress, the Hartshornes spent some four months traveling in France, Germany, Switzerland, Italy, and Spain. In the process Hartshorne was gathering material for his book, *The Philosophy and Psychology of Sensa-*

tion, which was published in 1934. In Italy he studied Giotto's frescoes and in Spain, paintings by El Greco.

Hartshorne's book on sensation represents a confluence of several streams in his thought—aesthetic, metaphysical, and psychological. At Harvard he had worked with the psychologists L. T. Troland, William Mc-Dougall, and Herbert S. Langfeld, and had immersed himself in the literature on sensation. In the book Hartshorne incorporated much that he had learned from his Harvard studies, but he contributed his own reflections in psychological theory as well. Though *The Philosophy and Psychology of Sensation* was his first book, he had been publishing articles since 1929. Since those early years, Hartshorne's literary output has been prodigious. He recently told a class: "My problem has never been 'publish or perish,' but 'teach or perish'!"

While at Chicago the Hartshornes maintained a simple cottage in the woods of the Indiana dunes, where Hartshorne spent many long weekends at work. In the years before World War II he would take the South Shore Electric to the cottage on a Friday afternoon and return just in time for classes on the following Tuesday. In those years the university held no classes on Saturday, and graduate courses did not meet on Monday, which was library day. As a youth, Hartshorne had lived only in small towns, and he loved the outdoors. The cottage provided a haven from the bustle and noise of Chicago.

Hartshorne taught steadily at the university, including many summers, until 1937, when he became visiting professor at Stanford University for the winter and spring quarters. On this visit to California the Hartshornes enjoyed many outings with the Sierra Club and made a six-weeks excursion into the high Sierra. They returned to California for ornithological study two years later.

In the year 1941/42 Hartshorne was exchange professor at the New School for Social Research. He was appointed to the faculty of the Divinity School of the University of Chicago in 1943 and thus held a joint appointment in philosophy and divinity. Students in the Divinity School had shown great interest in Hartshorne's courses. One of those students was Bernard Loomer, later Hartshorne's colleague as professor of theology and dean of the Divinity School. Looking back on Hartshorne's years with the Divinity School, Loomer recently remarked that Hartshorne managed to enrich every discussion in which he participated.

Hartshorne was among the half-dozen professors from the university who during 1948/49 went to Frankfurt, Germany, to teach at Goethe University. He taught there for six months but also lectured in other German cities, in Lund, Sweden, and at the Sorbonne. In 1952 he was Fulbright lecturer at the University of Melbourne and in addition spoke in Sydney, Adelaide, Hobart, and Canberra. The trip gave him the opportunity for research on bird song in Australia, Hawaii, and the Fiji Islands. In the Fiji Islands he managed to hear the Fijian warbler and gave the first description of its song ever written.

In 1955, after twenty-seven years at Chicago, Hartshorne became professor of philosophy at Emory University. He was at Emory seven years before going to the University of Texas in 1962. In 1958 Hartshorne was Fulbright lecturer in Japan's Kyoto University. He has been Ashbel Smith professor of philosophy at Texas since 1963 (the year in which he received the Lecomte du Noüy Award for *The Logic of Perfection*). He went to India in 1966 on a University of Texas research grant for the purpose of studying a problem in Hindu thought. There he lectured in several universities—for a month in Benares Hindu University—and from India he went to Hong Kong as a lecturer, then to Tokyo and Kyoto on a Fulbright lectureship secured by the Japanese. The following year Haverford College conferred on him an honorary degree, the Doctor of Humane Letters.

Hartshorne has written: "We learn from others, yet fresh impulses come chiefly from rather solitary reflections, courageously insisted upon."[1] His own rather solitary reflections have produced fresh impulses, and he has courageously insisted upon them. Of course, Hartshorne, though he is no stereotyped idealist, stands in the idealist tradition, as does process philosophy itself. In

---

1. Charles Hartshorne, "Method: In search of Nonrestrictive Conceptions," chap. 3 of Unpublished Manuscript used by Hartshorne in course at the University of Texas in 1965, p. 55. [The manuscript has been edited by Hartshorne since 1965 and the pagination has therefore been altered somewhat.] Hereafter, this work will be cited as Unpublished Manuscript.

his early years he fairly devoured the controversy between the idealists and their opponents. Possessed of the ability to "tear the heart out of a book" in short order, Hartshorne read all the idealists—German, British, and American. Thus, he was thoroughly familiar with the thought of Leibniz, Hegel, Berkeley, Bradley, Bosanquet, McTaggart, Royce, Hocking, Troland, and McDougall, and with some Buddhist and Hindu thinkers as well. He was just as familiar, however, with the critics of idealism, including Russell, Moore, Hartmann, James, Perry, Lewis, and Spaulding.

"Idealism," says Hartshorne, "got off on three wrong feet." There was Berkeley's subjectivism, Leibniz's atomism, and the absolute idealism of Hegel. But idealists hit upon a fundamental phenomenological truth: that sensation is inseparable from affective feeling. Whitehead saw this with great clarity and, as he told Hartshorne, was thus led to psychicalism. Hartshorne expounded that phenomenological truth in his first book, and he has never forsaken it. He has in effect expurgated idealism of mistakes which characterized it in the nineteenth century, mistakes which caused twentieth-century philosophers to turn from it. The task has required independence of mind—and greatness.

THE METHODOLOGICAL KEY

«««««««««««««««««««««

CHARLES HARTSHORNE CALLS HIS METAPHYSICAL SYSTEM neoclassical. Classical metaphysics, with a legacy of doctrines dating back to the Greeks, may be said to have ended with Hume and Kant.[1] Those two philosophers subjected classical metaphysical thought to searching criticism. Yet, neither Hume nor Kant offered a positive alternative to classical metaphysics, and neither challenged the legitimacy of the classical concepts as such. They questioned the foundations of the classical categories or limited their scope, but they did not free themselves from the traditional understanding of those categories. It is not difficult to see how Hume and Kant contributed to the modern decline of metaphysics. Skeptical attacks upon classical metaphysics can be taken (though mistakenly) to have undermined metaphysics as such—especially where no positive metaphysical alternative is offered. In the twentieth century a growing number of philosophers have sought to furnish such an alternative.

---

1. See Unpublished Manuscript, pp. 35–36.

Hartshorne, with his neoclassical metaphysics, may be numbered among the most notable of this group. He radically reinterprets the three fundamental notions of classical metaphysics—substance, causality, and deity. On analysis it can be seen that his reinterpretation employs the principle, discussed in this chapter, that a metaphysical truth is one whose denial results in incoherence. Indeed, use of the negative test may be taken as a key to the understanding of Hartshorne's philosophy. In the next chapter we will examine panpsychism, his answer to the classical substance doctrine, and in subsequent chapters we will consider the neoclassical view of time and of deity. Our contention is that in each case Hartshorne shows why honest efforts to falsify the neoclassical position are bound to fail.

For Hartshorne, the things of everyday experience— tables, stones, trees, and the rest—are realities, but not the primary realities. At a deeper level of analysis lie concrete particulars. Concealed from ordinary observation, these particulars compose (are the parts of) the things of everyday experience. Hartshorne's position, thus inelaborately stated, seems a mere commonplace of scientific theory with its doctrine of cells, molecules, and atoms. What immediately distinguishes his position, however, is the claim that concrete particulars are centers of feeling, essentially one with the experiencing subjects we know ourselves to be. Still, the distinction between an everyday thing and its concrete constituents does not represent a difference of modal status, for both the thing

and its constituents are contingent. Either exists thanks
to certain conditions, and nonexistence is conceivable of
the one as of the other. Hume pointed out that no state
of affairs obtains by logical necessity, that denial of the
existence of a state of affairs, even if false, need involve
no self-contradiction. As we ordinarily put it, the facts
are what they are, though they might have been otherwise. When we say it is a fact that X exists, we suggest
the contingency of X just as surely as when we say X
happens to exist. True, we also speak, for example, of
the "facts" of arithmetic, and in such cases no contingency is implied. Given this equivocation in the meaning
of facticity, it is advisable to stipulate that in this work
a fact will be construed as a state of affairs which excludes
all conceivable alternatives. The status of existing to the
exclusion of all conceivable alternatives is the very meaning of contingent actuality. "There is an elephant in
Cleveland." The statement asserts a contingency. It tells
us not only of something present in Cleveland but also
(though vaguely) of genuine options—namely, elephant-
free states of affairs—excluded from actualization in
Cleveland by the stated fact.

Basic to Hartshorne's view of contingency is the prem-
ise that every positive fact is a selection from a range
of disjunctive possibilities which could not all be realized
conjunctively.[2] Accordingly, such selection involves a

2. See Charles Hartshorne, *The Logic of Perfection and
Other Essays in Neoclassical Metaphysics* (La Salle, Ill.: Open
Court Publishing Company, 1962), p. 285.

correlative rejection, each yes a correlative no. Any positive state of affairs, then, since it excludes alternatives, has a negative side, and this negative side is itself a fact (and hence contingent). Goldwater did not win the presidential election of 1964. That, though negative, is a fact. A negative fact cannot be experienced—at least, not directly. It may nonetheless be conceived as a selection from the alternatives, as a condition or state of affairs which excludes options, any (though not all) of which might just as well have gained realization. But how can a negative fact exclude alternatives? Is such a fact anything more than a failure or absence of what might have been? Suppose the negative fact to be that it is not raining. Any state of weather involving rain (while logically conceivable) is then excluded from actualization. The exclusion is effected, however, only by the *presence* of some positive state of weather other than rain. This positive state is the correlate of the negative fact, its positive side. Thus, the theory of facticity leads us to conclude that just as every positive state of affairs must have a negative side, so every negative fact must have a positive side. The axiom of positivity——that no fact can be wholly negative, without positive bearing, but must be partly positive—is fundamental for Hartshorne. The axiom draws its force from the pairing of two points: (1) no fact, whether positive or negative, exists of necessity, and (2) alternative possibilities can be canceled only by a positive fact, not by a mere absence or privation.

One can readily see the relevance of these considerations for scientific procedure. If facts are all selections from conceivable alternatives, then factual information is possible only when an observer discovers which selections have actually been made—hence the reliance of the scientist on observation (and induction). Unaided logic is powerless to disclose which alternatives have been realized or which excluded, but a skilled and imaginative observer, on finding which have been realized, will also be aware of some of the exclusions. On the other hand, if every excluded or negative fact has a positive side, then the falsity of a scientific hypothesis can be established by the discovery of positive facts correlative with that falsity. Were wholly negative facts possible, some (perhaps all) hypotheses would be incapable of falsification, for no positive fact could be found to exclude or falsify them. But an unfalsifiable hypothesis would obtain, no matter what the facts were, and therefore would in no sense be hypothetical. A scientist proceeds, at least tacitly, on the axiom of positivity, since he assumes that if a hypothesis is false, there are positive facts whose discovery would disconfirm it.

A scientific hypothesis implies or predicts such and such facts *rather than others;* therefore if the latter turn up, the hypothesis is contradicted. Had Galileo found that above sea level water rises in a vacuum tube as high as or even higher than it does at or below sea level, his theory of barometric pressure would have been in serious trouble. As it happened, Galileo's expectations were not disappointed when his theory was brought to experi-

Perhaps so, but there are special difficulties. As Hartshorne explains, a metaphysical truth does not lend itself to diagrammatic representation in the way a truth of finite arithmetic does, nor to analysis by simple, noncontroversial rules of language.[6] Hence, the decision as to whether a given statement is a metaphysical truth cannot ordinarily be made on the grounds that it is or is not found to be analytic, in a narrow formal sense. Yet, something like the *ad absurdum* technique is possible. For consider. The denial of a metaphysical truth would represent an unqualified negation, since no fact could constitute the positive side of the denial, a metaphysical truth being one illustrated by any conceivable fact. In other words, a metaphysical truth is unexceptionally affirmative (exhibited in whatever facts obtain), and consequently its denial is unrestrictedly negative. Note that pure negativity is tantamount to absolute unknowability, for knowledge is possible if and only if there is something positive to be known. If, then, the denial of a statement yields a sheer negation or, equivalently, could never become a piece of knowledge, the denial is nonsensical, either trait indicating lack of meaning, and the statement denied may be taken as metaphysical truth.

Some philosophers seriously ask why there is something rather than nothing. Yet, to talk as though "no world at all" were a conceivable but unrealized fact is to conceal from oneself the pure negativity of the notion. For to say that nothing might actually exist is to treat

---

6. See Unpublished Manuscript, p. 3 and pp. 12–13.

nothing as though it were something rather than nothing, as though it might be realized to the exclusion of alternative states of affairs. Since this is nonsensical, the belief that bare nothing is a genuine alternative to existence (and to the principles of metaphysics) is false and necessarily so. Hartshorne argues this point persuasively.[7] The crux of his argument is that "nothing exists," while it can be falsified, can never be verified—since (1) a verifying experience would itself exist, and (2) no one could experience bare nothing; and that exclusive falsifiability means impossibility—since the truth of a statement implies at least the theoretical possibility of its confirmation.

Will the denial of any necessary statement whatever yield a sheer negation? If the necessary statement is nonmetaphysical, it is essentially negative, as we have said; therefore, its denial will not produce a sheer negation but instead a positive, existential assertion, one that is of course nonsensical. On the other hand, if the statement is metaphysical, its denial will yield a sheer negation, which will betray its lack of meaning through incoherence. For what is coherently conceivable is either possible or actual, while a sheer negation is neither the one nor the other; consequently, it is not coherently conceivable. Show that the denial of a positive, existential assertion is not coherently conceivable and you show that the assertion is a metaphysical truth. Hartshorne

7. See Charles Hartshorne, "Metaphysical Statements as Nonrestrictive and Existential," *The Review of Metaphysics* 12, no. 1 (September 1958): 35.

cautions, however, that a clear and certain determination as to whether a given a priori truth *is* positive may be beyond our cognitive powers.[8] It will scarcely be less difficult to determine whether its denial is wholly negative. This suggests that we may be unable finally to decide which variety of empty (nonempirical) truth we have on our hands, the "merely linguistic" or the metaphysical.

Now let us, in a summary, draw some of the threads together. A pure, unrestricted negation, since it represents what belongs to no possible state of affairs and is therefore contradicted by any conceivable fact, is noncontingently false—the negativity it asserts being an impossibility—and its meaning is wholly intralinguistic. Its contradictory, the positive form of noncontingency, is a metaphysical statement, which asserts something common to every possible state of affairs. The metaphysical statement is necessarily true, its truth being neutral to all existential alternatives. A contingent statement, unlike either form of the noncontingent, makes existence a question of fact rather than of meaning. It affirms the existence of something and at least by implication denies the existence of conceivable alternatives, or else it denies the existence of something and at least by implication affirms the existence of some conceivable alternative or other. It follows that whether an existential statement is contingent is simply a question of meaning, namely, a

---

8. See Hartshorne, *The Logic of Perfection*, p. 284.

question as to whether its truth and falsity are equi-possible.

Since metaphysical statements do not discriminate which possibilities are and which are not actualized, it is sometimes claimed that they tell us nothing about the world. Certainly they tell us nothing about the world if this means they fail to indicate how in some respect this actual world differs from other conceivable ones.[9] But if one wishes to be told about the world, and told with thoroughness, he may very well want to be informed, not only as to the world's distinctiveness, but as to features it shares with any world that might have been or may yet be. Only metaphysical statements can describe these features. One may argue that reference to features all possible worlds have in common is not descriptive or informative. But, as Hartshorne points out,[10] affirmations are no less true (and true of "this world") because they affirm that in which all possibilities agree, and surely the affirming of truth is descriptive or informative. If not, what words shall we use?

Hartshorne says that scientists investigate which among possible facts happen to be actual, metaphysicians which among verbally possible formulations of factuality are genuine.[11] Not facts but fact-as-such is the province

---

9. See Unpublished Manuscript, p. 11.

10. See ibid.

11. See ibid., p. 33; see also Charles Hartshorne, *Reality as Social Process: Studies in Metaphysics and Religion* (Glencoe, Ill.: Free Press, 1953), p. 29.

of metaphysics. A double-barreled objection may be leveled at this view of its province. On the one hand, it may be objected that metaphysics cannot be confined to fact-as-such, its task being to treat being qua being. On the other hand, it may be objected that "fact-as-such" is so general as to swallow up distinctions which are essential to meaning. The following reply may help answer these objections. Metaphysics, or the study of fact-as-such, is primarily the theory of concreteness, the concrete being reality in its fullness or inclusiveness. Now, the investigation of factuality, granting that it preserves the basic forms of contrast within the concrete, omits consideration of no dimension of being as such. Moreover, in preserving these basic forms of contrast, it avoids obliterating indispensable distinctions and thereby falling into meaninglessness.

The basic forms of contrast are distinctions of logical type. The complete generality of metaphysics does not imply indifference to the distinction between the concrete and the abstract, that is, between the concrete and its aspects or constituents; indeed, a theory of concreteness must *include* a theory of abstractness. Accordingly, Hartshorne distinguishes the event—the fully concrete—from the individual, the group, and the abstract quality. He regards the existential contrast between God and the creatures as a unique logical-type distinction, one within a logical type, that of individuality.

The acknowledgment of logical levels, each of the higher levels an abstraction from the concrete, in no way compromises the principle that denial of a metaphysical truth amounts to a sheer negation and is unknowable (can never be known to be true). Granted, what *distinguishes* one level from those that are more abstract will have no applicability to them. It should not be supposed, for example, that blue and triangularity—since they exist—are subjects with feelings. No panpsychist, not even the most fanciful or fervent, ever intended such absurdity. What the panpsychist intends is that nothing having full concreteness is totally dead and insentient. Yet, each level, taken intensionally or conceptually, implies each of the others, metaphysical truth being a unity of logically interdependent structures. For concreteness and abstractness (including each of its basic forms) are ideas which each entail the other. It follows that one cannot deny only part of the metaphysical net work. To deny any of it is in truth to deny the whole of it.

Hartshorne does not contend that nonfalsifiability is a simple, foolproof test of a metaphysical claim. Issues in metaphysics are too subtle and complex—and human beings too willing to believe as they please. The brightest hope of finding metaphysical truth is to compare a theory and its (exhaustively enumerated) alternatives, giving each a full and fair hearing. The decision for one among the options would not imply that it was free from all difficulties. Such a decision would imply only that the difficulties connected with the chosen option were relatively less serious, some being due to remediable unclarity, others to intricacy in the ideas, and still others to factors such as personal bias. However, a comparative study of this sort will make prominent use of the negative test—falsifiability—since in metaphysics, as in science, we move toward truth indirectly, by failure of honest efforts to falsify.[12]

12. See Unpublished Manuscript, p. 28.

3

PANPSYCHISM

«««««««««««««««««««««

ARISTOTLE HELD THAT EVERYTHING IN THE NATURAL WORLD may be classified according to a tripartite scheme.[1] First (and highest) are the animals—possessed of souls; in second place, the plants—also besouled; and finally, material bodies—wholly inanimate. There is nothing very startling about this classification. It is as much a piece of common sense as it is a philosophical doctrine. Indeed, all of us have adopted it, more or less. But can a philosopher go beyond the appeal to common sense in justifying his view that nature is composed of animals, plants, and inanimate objects? In particular, can he provide convincing reasons for believing that one stratum of nature is utterly lifeless?

Aristotle would probably have insisted that any man with good healthy sense organs can discover for himself that much of the natural world is simply inanimate ma-

---

1. See Hartshorne's discussion of the scheme in his "Present Prospects for Metaphysics," *The Monist* 47, no. 2 (Winter 1963): 197–201.

terial. The prior question, however, is whether sense perception should be *trusted* to settle the matter. We rely upon our senses to adjudicate many questions. For example, a young man who is curious as to whether a certain girl is wearing an engagement ring may glance at the girl's hand to find out if a ring is present. We would think it strange if the young man reported that he had gotten a good, close look at her hand—in broad daylight, with his better-than-normal vision, etc.—but was yet unsure whether she was wearing a ring.

A table certainly looks lifeless, but is that ground enough to conclude that it is inanimate through and through? Should the failure to perceive life in a physical object be taken as proof that none is there? Aristotle assumed that perception is competent to judge the matter. But perhaps perception should not be expected to reveal the whole truth about tables or other seemingly dead objects. If not, then Aristotle had no right to take his failure to detect (perceive) life in certain objects and convert that failure into a success, into a declaration that those objects are wholly inanimate.[2] In short, Aristotle did not *know* that one great division of the natural world is soulless and dead. Nor does anyone else know this.

Aristotle's rather naïve reliance on sense perception cannot be excused on the ground that the ancient Greeks were not sophisticated enough to be critical about sensation. Plato certainly did not trust the senses to disclose

2. See ibid., pp. 200–201.

reality. Moreover, the Greek atomists, whom Aristotle knew well enough, were boldly critical of sensation. They denied that an observer can perceive the constituent parts of a physical object. The ultimate constituents, they held, are imperceptibly small. Here was a remarkable theory, an atomic theory, enunciated centuries before the rise of modern science. What the atomists were saying, in effect, was that we never perceive the single, the unitary, the individual, when we examine a physical object. A table, to take our example, is really a group; it is a many, not a one. And perception puts us in touch with the group— but only with the group as a totality and never with the atomic parts composing it. It is as though the physical object perceived were a pile of sand whose individual grains escaped detection.

The atomists made one unfortunate leap in the dark: they supposed that the microindividuals, the atoms, were *like* the perceived aggregates. Hence, they concluded that the units of physical reality are bits of lifeless stuff, and they tried to conceive the whole universe as built up from and reducible to these inanimate units. We should not judge their materialism too harshly. After all, "the incomparable Mr. Newton" adopted a quite similar view, and only in recent times has that view been discarded as the final word. Nonetheless, it is not safe to assume that we can infer the character of the imperceptible individuals which compose a group from an empirical examination of the group. A rock—as an aggregate—may be inert and dead, but this does not settle the question as to whether its component parts are. Appearances *are* deceiving. And the rock, to all appearances passive and inanimate, may veil from view the life and dynamism of its individual constituents.

Imagine a man in a blimp high over a crowded football stadium. Gazing down, he would probably be unable to discriminate individuals below but would see the crowd as a mass, characterized perhaps by patches or patterns of color. No one would mistake such a mass phenomenon for a concrete individual, nor assume that its character was like that of the individual spectators in the stands. Again: from a distance a swarm of bees flying above the treetops might look like a small, dark cloud—so much inert stuff—the individual agency of the member-bees being deceptively hidden from view. And our rock, is it not a swarm too? The rock-swarm itself is dead enough—dead as a doornail—but this is so because it is a group rather than an individual. Dead men tell no tales, and dead rock-swarms tell nothing to ordinary perceivers about their living individual members.

But at this point the case is far from closed. Perhaps the atomists were hasty in supposing that the individual components of physical reality are each instances of "mere matter." Even so, what grounds have we for saying that these components are living? It is important to refer here to Leibniz,[3] who reasoned that if all visible

---

3. See Hartshorne, "Structure of Metaphysics," p. 235, as well as Unpublished Manuscript, pp. 64–65.

things are made up of parts too small to be discerned individually, then we have no visual acquaintance with any instance of individuality—unless the parts of a thing are themselves so interdependent as to form a dynamic unity and hence an individual. Vertebrate animals such as "I myself" do constitute such unities. Indeed, the only individuals we see in any direct sense (except for insects or worms) are vertebrates. Yet, we fail to discern their individuality fully, so that even here individuality escapes us. However, in a nonsensory mode of experience, namely, immediate memory or introspection, we know ourselves as individuals, not merely as aggregates of parts, themselves individually unknown. And what we in mnemonic self-awareness experience is our just past unity of feeling or experience. Hence, as Leibniz concluded, introspective experience furnishes not only our sole means of intuiting individuality but the principle of individuality itself. Accordingly, he conceived monads as unities of experience, in analogy not with visible objects but with the data we find in our own self-experience.

So (1) if a physical object such as a rock is not itself an individual but merely a mosaic of imperceptible individuals, and (2) if the only individuals we know are unities of experience—can the ultimate, simple individuals be other than animate and sentient? To be sure, the concrete singulars which comprise a physical object are not (necessarily) animal, but they may by extrapolation be conceived as units of experience responsible in part for their own formation. We need not attribute to those individuals characteristics which belong to the higher levels of experience—consciousness or language, for example. It is arbitrary to assert that all experience must be of the developed, complex human sort. Experience can be as flexible as anything imaginable. Even within human experience there is a bewildering variety of ranges, degrees, and levels. Some of our memories are short, others sweep far back into the past. At times, our experience is intense and concentrated; then again, we lapse into reverie or into nearly dreamless sleep. We reason, we enjoy, we anticipate, we choose—in multiformity. Do we really suppose there is some lowest limit in nature, below which there is just insentient, lifeless stuff?[4]

Still, how can we be *sure* that there are no dead, insentient individuals? Of course, we cannot be sure, but we can build a reasonable case. One who claims that part of nature is wholly dead is asserting that a certain absence or privation characterizes the part of nature in question. For to say that an object is inanimate is really to say what it *lacks:* it is to say that it is not living, not feeling, not hoping, not remembering, not enjoying, and so forth. Indefinable as it may be, experience is known to us directly. We *have* experience. We are acquainted with a wide variety of its forms. But how do we know its absence? Or more generally, how do we know a negative fact?

---

4. See Hartshorne, *The Logic of Perfection*, p. 225 and p. 309.

Plato spoke of sophists who denied that they told falsehoods and to support their denial gave the following argument: to utter a falsehood would be to say what is not; but what is not is nothing at all, and one cannot say nothing at all, for to speak is to say *something*. As Plato saw, the argument turns on the supposition that there are *sheer* absences or privations, of which falsehood is an instance. According to Hartshorne's axiom of positivity, a negative fact is never completely negative— a hole or vacuum in reality—but always implies or involves certain positive facts. Indeed, we become cognizant of negative facts by way of the positive facts. For the latter exclude or negate possible states of affairs which might otherwise have obtained. We cite the positive facts, which we experience, as evidence for the absence of the excluded or negative facts.

What positive evidence can we cite as testimony to the absence of life in physical objects? Descartes thought that physical bodies are spatially extended while mind is not. Following Descartes's doctrine, we might argue that the extendedness of an entity, being incompatible with life or feeling, is a positive fact whose presence proves that life or feeling is absent. The trouble with this argument is simply that Descartes was wrong in supposing mind to be unextended.[5] A given experience is not at

5. See Hartshorne, "Structure of Metaphysics," p. 237; also see "Interrogation of Charles Hartshorne (conducted by William Alston)," in *Philosophical Interrogations*, ed. Sydney and Beatrice Rome (New York: Holt, Rinehart and Winston, 1964), p. 351; and Unpublished Manuscript, pp. 76–77.

some dimensionless point—nor is it nowhere at all.[6] And it is not just anywhere you please. As many philosophers have seen, experience has a social structure: an experience is always *of* something else. Its relation to that other gives it a regional spread, a spatial dimensionality or extendedness.[7]

Perhaps it will be said that predictability is evidence for lifeless matter. But this is unconvincing. In the first place, there is no reason to suppose that life or experience cannot exist in a form elementary enough for prediction to be successful. The randomness or spontaneity of life need not be impressive and may in some cases be negligible. In the second place, the universal predictability of nature is no longer accepted by physicists as a truism. The behavior of a mass or aggregate can in most cases be predicted fairly well—for example, the behavior of a weight dropped from the Leaning Tower. But the subatomic constituents of that weight are not so tame and docile. Indeed, we are hearing more and more these days about unexpected (almost fantastic) antics at the subatomic level. Statistics work, with varying degrees of success, on groups; but with varying degrees of failure on individuals—microindividuals included. In the third place, predictability is not only com-

---

6. See Hartshorne, *Reality as Social Process*, pp. 36–37; his *The Logic of Perfection*, p. 201; and "Interrogation of Charles Hartshorne," p. 335.

7. See Hartshorne, "Structure of Metaphysics," p. 237, and "Interrogation of Charles Hartshorne," p. 335.

patible with psychicalism—as order is with freedom—
but really requires it in order to be understood. There
could be no world without order and regularity. But
why should the world be law-abiding—if it is, or insofar
as it is, mere dead matter? That seems unintelligible. A
sentient entity is not only inventive, but sensitive to
influence. Indeed, there is no appropriate way of conceiving the influence of one thing on another except in
terms of the latter's sensitivity to the former. Hence, if
the world in each of its concretions is sentient, its
predictability can be explained by reference to the influence (and thus the control) exerted by one member
over others, ultimately by God over all.

If extendedness and predictability cannot be taken
as evidence for mere dead matter, surely no positive trait
can be. And if not, then no individual entity can be
known to be lifeless. Thus, materialism is false in some
cases—for there *are* living, experiencing beings—and cannot be known to be true *as a fundamental interpretation*
in any case. Or putting it another way, psychicalism is
true in some cases and could not be known to be false *as
a fundamental interpretation* in any case. Using the
methodological key, we may draw the conclusion that
materialism, since it involves sheer negation, is necessarily false and psychicalism therefore a metaphysical
truth.

Taken as a fundamental interpretation of concrete
reality, psychicalism is capable of doing justice to the
concerns of materialism (but not materialism to those of

psychicalism). For, as Hartshorne points out, extension and experience are not logically exclusive of one another —like "becomes" and "does not become," nor are they competitive on the same level of concreteness—like red and green.[8] Rather, experience *embraces* size, shape, motion, etc., as its phenomenal, measurable aspects. Writes Hartshorne: "'Mind' and 'matter' are not two ultimately different sorts of entity but, rather, two ways of describing a reality that has many levels of organization. The 'mind' way I take to be more final and inclusive, so that my position is the opposite of materialism."[9] Thus, the claim that every concrete entity is at least sentient does not imply that it lacks extension but that its extension is *within* its sentient wholeness.

The materialistic opposite of Hartshorne's position, since it is the denial of sentient-and-extended, can be seen clearly in its negativity. It fastens on the latter part of the conjunction and declares it to be the whole story. Does the "insentience of singulars," involving as it does pure negativity, contain incoherence? Yes, all the incoherence of mistaking the abstract for the concrete, a mistake which Whitehead calls "the Fallacy of Misplaced Concreteness." For "mere matter" is an abstraction from the concreteness of experience, the residuum of omission from its positivity. As Leibniz argued against Descartes,[10] extension is a pattern of geometrical relationships, and

---

8. See Unpublished Manuscript, pp. 76–77.
9. Hartshorne, *The Logic of Perfection*, p. 217.
10. See Unpublished Manuscript, p. 77.

in itself a pattern is merely a type or class, not a particular entity at all.[11] *Of what* is extension the pattern?
The world is certainly no "bloodless dance of categories"
(Bradley's phrase, quoted by Whitehead).[12] Descartes
tacitly admits this, for he thinks of the modes of extension, the "primary qualities," as inhering in substance.
Scientific analysis has shown that the "substance" of a
physical object is "the persistence of certain forms (sta-
tistically, rather than absolutely, persistent) exhibited by
microscopic events." [13]   But simply on philosophical
grounds, it can be seen that an enduring stuff that supports qualities but is itself free of any is a fiction. The
only way to escape the "bloodless dance," on the one
hand, and a fictional substrate, on the other, is to view
the modes of extension as the social structure of feeling.[14]
Obviously, the empiricist (sensationalist) can never go
beyond materialism in the direction of either the substance doctrine or psychicalism; he can only add "secondary qualities" to the chronogcometric.

By distinguishing feelings from structures (and relations) that characterize them, the psychicalist can explain
self-identity through time and space. A thing or person
is not an "unchanging subject of change" but a persisting
pattern instantiated by a society of feeling-events. Only

11. See Hartshorne, *Reality as Social Process,* p. 80.
12. See Alfred North Whitehead, *Modes of Thought* (New
York: Macmillan Company, 1938), p. 197.
13. Hartshorne, *The Logic of Perfection,* p. 222.
14. See "Interrogation of Charles Hartshorne," p. 351.

feeling-events are fully concrete.[15] They are therefore on a different level, logically and metaphysically, from things or persons. Hartshorne has long propounded this all-important distinction between the actual and the existential, between occurrences and endurances.[16] (It is indispensable to his doctrine of God, enabling him to avoid choosing between God the eternal and God the temporal.) Dualism, rather than doing away with the incoherence of taking extension as concrete, adds its own peculiar form of incoherence. For though it recognizes both mind and matter, it makes them both concrete. Hence, it brings down on its head the insoluble problem of the relation between two domains radically unlike one another. The classic form of this problem is how to conceive the interaction of mind and body—or even the localization of the mind in the body.[17]

Another form of the same problem is posed by evolutionary theory. The evolvement of life and mind is unintelligible if in the final analysis nature is nothing more than tiny, lifeless BB's. For on these terms evolution would mean that the later products of the process were wholly different in nature from their sources, the qualitative having arisen from the quantitative. Causes need not entail their effects, but they must make them

---

15. See Hartshorne, "Structure of Metaphysics," p. 230.

16. See Hartshorne, *Reality as Social Process*, pp. 204–7; his "Structure of Metaphysics," p. 230; his *The Logic of Perfection*, p. 218; and his "Necessity," *The Review of Metaphysics* 21, no. 2 (December 1967): 291.

17. See Hartshorne, *The Logic of Perfection*, pp. 224–26.

possible. One may, of course, have recourse to sheer emergence—or to miracle. But in either case, explanation is sacrificed. We gain explanatory power by conceiving the lower levels of nature, all the way down, to have affinity with the higher. Panpsychism provides the only way of conceiving that affinity, unless one chooses to purchase it negatively, by wholesale denial of life and mind. In the latter case, we avoid the Scylla of dualism only to be faced with the Charybdis of materialism. Neither materialism nor dualism offers a coherent account of cause or time. Since the days of Hume, philosophers have puzzled over the question as to whether there is any basis for attributing causation to things in nature. Even more fundamental is the question of the objectivity of time, for causation presupposes the temporal modes. Hume was right: all we ever see in empirical observations of nature is one thing (which we call the cause) followed by another (which we call the effect); never do we get a glimpse of causation itself. Only when we take account of nonsensory awareness, in the experience of our own bodies and personal pasts, do we transcend the abstract "this, then that" and find the present being shaped by its retrospection of past events. A feeling is never its *own* datum, though it can be a datum for subsequent feelings.[18] It is the social structure of feeling, the asymmetrical feeling of other (past) feeling, that provides the experiential basis of the temporal-

18. See ibid., p. 227.

causal structure. "The leaf resting on the ground 'has fallen' there, but this having-fallen, where is it, as a property of the leaf?" [19] Surely nowhere—if there is no sentience in the leaf. For what is the past to mere matter?[20] Could it be that the so-called inanimate world holds the past within its present—and is thereby causally influenced—through something akin to memory? How else can one thing take account of something antecedent to itself? How else can the temporal-causal structure of nature be conceived? In the next chapter we will present the Hartshornian interpretation of this structure.

One may restrict himself to a materialistic view for methodological purposes. Hartshorne remarks: "I recognize that the material mode of description is that part of the complete mode which is capable of scientific precision and that, accordingly, 'methodological materialism,' or the restriction of attention to this mode, is a natural bias among scientists." [21] But note, materialism does not suffice as a complete picture of how things are. It is true—but only at some level, and not at the concrete level at that—so it is not the whole truth about the world nor even part of the truth about the concrete as such, and when so taken it manifests the incoherence of a denial of metaphysical truth.

---

19. Hartshorne, *Reality as Social Process*, p. 78.
20. See Charles Hartshorne and William L. Reese, *Philosophers Speak of God* (Chicago: University of Chicago Press, 1953), pp. 91–92.
21. Hartshorne, *The Logic of Perfection*, p. 217.

DETERMINISM AND THE
CREATIONIST VIEW OF TIME

ONE IDEAL OF CLASSICAL THOUGHT IS THAT EVENTS CAN BE explained by reference to their causes. Hartshorne does not deny that events have causes; indeed, he insists that they do.[1] But he asks whether the causes of an event can *fully* account for that event. If one replies affirmatively here, he has adopted the position of classical determinism. It is, as Hartshorne says,[2] an absolutistic position: it holds that the causal conditions of any event require that event in all its detail and eliminate the possibility of any other event or any other detail of that event. Accordingly, nothing at all can be otherwise, since everything is necessitated by its antecedent conditions. One aim of science, in this view, is to discover what will be from what has been and is, to foresee or predict future happenings on the basis of their causal antecedents.

If determinism is metaphysically false, it must involve some failure in meaning, some absurdity or self-contra-

---

1. See Hartshorne, *The Logic of Perfection*, p. 162.
2. See ibid., p. 165.

diction. But if this is so, few philosophers seem to have noticed. Hartshorne, however, asserts that the idea of predictability, when turned into an absolute, is senseless.[3] Absolute tidiness, he contends, is a contradiction in terms.[4] His own position, that causes or conditions limit more or less sharply what can happen, but never exhaustively determine what will happen,[5] can claim certification as a metaphysical truth if determinism—its contradictory—can be shown to be nonsensical. But can this be shown? Determinism has at times been defended precisely on the ground that it preserves rationality. What a queer, unintelligible world it would be, so runs the argument, if things could unpredictably leap into existence, surprising even one who had full knowledge of their antecedents. No, the only reasonable doctrine is that things are implicit in their causes; and we really explain what happens only by analyzing these causes. But can we agree that to explain anything we must show it to be deducible from something else? Indeed, do we not also reach understanding of a thing when we see that it does *not* follow from something else?[6] No one need deny that causes, though not sufficient conditions of their effects, are nonetheless necessary conditions of them. A tree cannot exist without sun, soil, and water (or their equivalents), but these elements alone cannot produce it.

---

3. See ibid., p. 172.
4. See Hartshorne, *Reality as Social Process*, p. 97.
5. See Hartshorne, *The Logic of Perfection*, pp. 163–64.
6. See Hartshorne, *Reality as Social Process*, p. 90.

An explanation of the tree would hardly involve a demonstration of its inevitability—given certain causes. To learn how a tree might come into being, to ascertain what conditions would be required for its germination and growth, is explanation enough. Is there really any other form of explanation (that is, any form besides giving an account of the conditions which make something possible), any other meaning to the term? Are there really instances where events in all their detail have been deduced from their antecedents? If not, why use deduction as the model of explanation? The determinist will perhaps admit that we never know an event as fully deducible from its causes, that we do not in this sense possess an explanation of it. But, as Hartshorne points out,[7] the determinist will assert the cryptotheological dogma that if we knew the causes of the event with perfect adequacy, we should then know the event as an implication of those causes and thus possess its explanation.

Since it is not man's lot to be omniscient about an event and its causes, observation can never guarantee the zero of irregularity required by the determinist thesis. Indeed, within a margin of error, whatever its magnitude, there is an infinity of possible values for randomness; therefore, the probability that this value is exactly zero

---

7. See Charles Hartshorne, "Contingency and the New Era in Metaphysics (I) ," *The Journal of Philosophy* 29, no. 16 (August 1932): 429.

is one over infinity.[8] Thus, not only is determinism unknowable so far as any human observer is concerned, there is an infinite improbability of it. The intriguing question, however, is whether determinism makes sense, whether it even could provide the explanation of a happening. As already indicated, Hartshorne's conviction is that the rational coherence of the world is destroyed, not sustained, by determinism. The central thrust of his argument is that determinism obliterates temporal succession, reducing reality to a great system in which, on analysis, everything is seen to entail everything else, and this, Hartshorne sees, is nonsense.

Knowledge is "agreement with reality." If so, knowledge of an event via its antecedents is cognitive agreement with that event. On the deterministic hypothesis, an event would hold no secrets from an ideal knower of its antecedents; and to such a knower, cognitive agreement with the event would be complete and exhaustive. But could there ever be such agreement were the event in all its particularity not there to be known? A wholly determinate cognition of some concrete event X cannot exist without X, the term or object of the cognitive relation. Yet, if to the ideal knower, X is present without remainder, and present because total knowledge of its antecedents reveals it totally, X is future (and its causes antecedent to it) only for our deficient human knowledge. Since determinism exempts no event from

8. This point was made by Peirce. See Hartshorne's discussion, ibid., p. 426.

the rule that a thing is absolutely knowable through its causes, all "future" events are—and ever have been—present and available to any who might have the eyes to see deeply enough into the causes of things. This implication—that "future" events are not yet to be but are already—casts a dark shadow of suspicion upon the deterministic doctrine.

The determinist may insist that to know *what* anything is—no matter how detailed the knowledge—is not to know *that* it is. Though one foreknew all features of some event, that event would still be future, since it would not yet have occurred. Hartshorne, agreeing with Whitehead, holds that definiteness *is* actuality.[9] To deny that a thing qua actual *is* its full definiteness or particularity is to commit oneself to the position that actuality is a totally featureless something, a sheer surd—even for an omniscient knower.[10] On this view, the causes of an event do not furnish its actuality. What then do they furnish? One is tempted to answer that they furnish its possibility. But consider. On the determinist thesis, the possibility of an event is without alternative. A possibility without alternative is, however, no possibility, since possibility is alternativeness. Something without alternative can only be a necessity. The determinist is claiming, then, that the causes of a concrete event X furnish its necessity—but not its actuality. How can the knowable

---

9. See Hartshorne, *Reality as Social Process*, p. 88 and p. 94.

10. See Hartshorne, *The Logic of Perfection*, p. 165.

features of the event, furnished by its causes, be necessary yet not actual? If causal conditions exclude all but one particular shade of blue as the color of a table, it will of course be that shade of blue. But the necessity is not merely that the table is destined to have that color. The shade of blue is here and now fully definite without alternative, available to the ideal knower of causes. What then does it mean to say that the table is not yet actually that shade? Actualization—whatever it is—adds no quality, no feature, to a thing, all its aspects being fully discoverable in its causes. If so, actualization of a certain shade of blue as the color of a table is not the realization of some visible or otherwise experienceable character of the table (since this would mean the addition of some definiteness). So it seems that the table is already that shade of blue, though not actually! But if one could see a table with a certain blue coloring, what would it mean to say it was not actually blue? Surely the actuality of a thing is inseparable from its determinate character, if indeed actuality and determinateness are not equivalent or identical.

The determinist, then, avoids collapsing possibility into actuality only by holding that an event is more than its determinate particularity and that this more is not included among its causes. We have questioned whether this doctrine is sound. Suppose we now take a different tack and ask whether the doctrine is really consonant with determinism. If a happening is always more than its causes provide, then it is not absolutely determined. For the event is not wholly deducible from its causes. Is the more—that is, the actuality of the occurrence—uncaused? Is it inexplicable? Does it leap forth creatively, unpredictably? Obviously, the doctrine that a happening is not exhausted by its causes is in truth a doctrine of contingency, subtly bootlegged into the determinist hypothesis in order to preserve an element of genuine futurity. Causes either totally account for their effects or they do not. If not, then determinism as an absolute is untenable.

Assume absolute determinism and you are stuck with the following problem: if causes totally account for their effects, that is, if they are sufficient conditions of those effects, then those effects are all given with their causes. And this implies that the whole of reality is eternal—unless, contrary to the deterministic hypothesis, there is a "first" cause, a cause wholly without cause, purely contingent, purely chance, from which all effects are deducible. In any case, all events are given "at once," whether eternally or with the first cause; they are not successive. As we have seen, a determinist who tries to escape this consequence by appealing to the notion that some factor called "actual occurrence" is absent from an event's causes is abandoning the determinist position. For, again, what brings about or causes an "actual occurrence"? Surely nothing does if it is not implied by the causes of the occurrence, and we then have an undetermined and novel factor. On the other hand, if caused, it must already be present in its causes, since causes are supposed to determine absolutely.

Of course, the crucial question is whether it makes sense to speak of qualities strictly entailed by causes but not yet actual. When the sufficient conditions of a thing obtain, what could explain its absence? Hartshorne holds that necessities are factors common to a set of possibilities, since any possibility that is actualized will involve those factors.[11] And, for him, the causal conditions of an event supply its possibility and therefore impose certain necessities upon it. Determinism, however, can make no use of such a conception of necessity, for by squeezing out all contingency (thus revealing its basic negativity), it eliminates possibility, leaving only the nonoptional, the necessary, but without indefiniteness. Hartshorne calls attention to Peirce's observation that absolute determinism amounts to sheer nominalism, since it leaves nothing indefinite and thus destroys the distinction between universal and particular (as well as that between possible and actual).[12]

Note that each link in the chain of causes and effects, deterministically understood, is unconditionally necessary. A particular follows necessarily from its causes, and

---

11. See Hartshorne, *Reality as Social Process,* p. 86, and his *The Logic of Perfection,* p. 174.
12. See Charles Hartshorne, "Contingency and the New Era in Metaphysics (II)," *The Journal of Philosophy* 29, no. 17 (August 1932): 458.

they in turn from theirs. So, unless one has recourse to the theory of a "first" cause, which would of course mean a purely free decision, there is nothing hypothetical about any event. Clearly, it follows, as Hartshorne says,[13] that temporal direction is thereby eliminated, for a necessity is implied by anything, and since all particulars are supposedly necessary, all are implied by all others. Nothing is prior to anything else, so that there is no backward or forward at all. The "past" is as much explained by the "present" as vice versa. Any item at all implies all items in the cosmos—they are all internal to it—so that to understand anything would require understanding of everything. We can now appreciate the cogency of Bergson's point, that time if it is not creative is nothing.[14] Hartshorne declares that this point is still poorly digested in philosophy. Of course, this implies that the meaning of determinism has been poorly digested. Once one grasps that meaning, he faces a choice between the deterministic denial of all external relations (hence, of plurality) and the affirmation of at least some external relations. To adopt the latter position is to grant elements of novelty, elements not furnished by any causal conditions; it is to preserve difference and plurality, and hence temporal succession and direction.

How is such a choice to be made? One may try to

---

13. See Hartshorne, "Contingency and the New Era in Metaphysics (I)," pp. 422–23.
14. Hartshorne refers to the point in his *Reality as Social Process*, p. 201, and in his *The Logic of Perfection*, p. 165.

falsify the determinist-necessitarian position by reference to facts. He may appeal to his experience of contingency not only in the case of free and responsible moral acts but in the very temporal process itself. But if determinism is false, it is false not because it conflicts with certain observed data but because, being somehow nonsensical, it could never be true. Is determinism, even if it implies a Parmenidean world, a nonsensical doctrine? One way of stating the determinist position is to affirm that a thing's causes, no matter how remote, squeeze out all alternatives, all options, to that thing and thus make it necessary. Is there an intelligible account of this absolute extrusion of possibilities? How can one thing utterly and completely define another? Whether this can be explained or not, the determinist holds that it is so. A man may suppose that he could have been taller or shorter than he is. But he is mistaken in his supposition; neither option is genuine. If, however, there could have been no state of affairs but the one given, if every alternative is bogus, it follows that "logical possibilities" are really impossible, for what simply cannot be is not possible. Thus, to entertain notions as to what *might* have been or what *may* be is to lapse into sheer confusion. An alternative to what is necessary, that is, without alternative, is not consistently conceivable. Options then are unthinkable, inconceivable. We are left with a wholly necessary world. It is a strictly metaphysical world, a world which, like the medieval deity, is *actus purus*.

Does this make sense? In ordinary parlance, we

usually use the term "necessary" in a relative sense: X is not simply necessary, but necessary to or for or in respect to something else. But in the history of philosophy the term is often applied—to God, to principles, or even to the world—in a way that seems direct and nonrelative. Even in these cases, however, there is an implicit—albeit an abstract—kind of relativity. For on analysis the concept necessity is seen to involve the contrasting concept contingency. Hartshorne points out that every basic category requires for its own meaning contrast with its polar opposite.[15] If so, the collapse of such a contrast would mean the collapse of meaning for both poles. Determinism, in reducing everything to necessity, collapses the contrast upon which both terms, possible and necessary, depend and thus destroys the meaning of both with a single blow. This becomes evident to one who inquires into the meaning of "necessary." For, as he finds, to be necessary is to be without alternative. Therefore, if it is absurd to speak of alternatives, it is absurd to speak of that whose definition requires the concept of alternatives, of that which is the alternative to alternatives.

Hartshorne's principle of polarity enables us to see that the necessitarianism implicit in determinism is untenable simply because it does not make sense. The contrary absolute, unrestricted freedom, makes no better sense. Each of the following points entails this con-

---

15. See Hartshorne, *Reality as Social Process*, p. 86.

clusion. (1) As Hartshorne has often pointed out,[16] one state of affairs will always be incompatible with others, and therefore they cannot all be realized together. To be anything at all, an entity must be *this* rather than *that*, or *that* rather than *this*. Once more, then, we come to the thesis that actuality involves definiteness. (2) Moreover, alternative states of affairs are not absolutely diverse and different from one another. In fact, it is inconceivable that they should not share some factors in common, sameness and difference being themselves polar concepts. This means that within a range of possibilities, there will be certain invariants, ingredients pervading the range without possible alternative. (3) In addition, if there are several centers of freedom, no one of them can possess unlimited freedom, since each will limit the other. Hartshorne has argued cogently that power, by its very nature, is distributed and cannot be absolutely monopolized.[17] Granting this, it follows that any center of freedom will be limited, for it will always be one among others.

The position Hartshorne adopts is opposed to both absolutes, that of sheer necessity and that of unrestricted freedom; it may be called relative indeterminism, but this, as he remarks,[18] is at the same time relative deter-

---

16. See, for example, Hartshorne, *The Logic of Perfection*, pp. 284–85.

17. See Hartshorne, "Omnipotence," in *An Encyclopedia of Religion*, ed. Vergilius Ferm (Patterson, N.J.: Littlefield, Adams and Co., 1959), pp. 545–46.

18. See Hartshorne, *The Logic of Perfection*, p. 174.

minism. If neither absolute makes sense and the respective contradictories—some freedom and some necessity— can be seen as facets of a single position, namely, relative indeterminism (or relative determinism), it follows that this position cannot be false, its denial being all but verbally impossible, but must be metaphysically true. Here we have an example of the way Hartshorne's method operates, the negative, *ad absurdum* test being used to establish a position by discrediting its denial. We have already indicated how Hartshorne conceives the togetherness of freedom and necessity. The necessary, as he explains, is that which pervades a range of chances of possibilities. Will the events of tomorrow have such and such a character? Today's real possibilities for tomorrow may *all* include that character, in which case it cannot but occur. But if *none* of those possibilities include the character, it simply cannot be realized tomorrow.[19] Of course, some of the possibilities may include while others exclude the character, in which case it may occur, though it need not. The first case is that in which conditions for the occurrence of the character are sufficient: its occurrence is inevitable, determined. In the second case, not

19. See Charles Hartshorne, *Man's Vision of God and The Logic of Theism* (Chicago: Willett, Clark and Company, 1941), pp. 139–40; see also Charles Hartshorne, *Anselm's Discovery: A Re-examination of the Ontological Proof for God's Existence* (La Salle, Ill.: Open Court Publishing Company, 1965), p. 61, as well as Charles Hartshorne, "Causal Necessities: An Alternative to Hume," *The Philosophical Review* 63, no. 4 (October 1954): 487.

even the necessary conditions of its occurrence are present, while in the third the necessary conditions are present to some but not to all the possibilities and therefore the conditions are not sufficient for its occurrence. In short, necessity is ingredient in possibility; it is that wherein a set of possibilities agree.[20]

Given this background, we can see that every event, no matter how fresh and novel, inherits from its causal conditions, some elements of this inheritance being inescapable, regardless of which event is actualized from those conditions. Time is then an order of asymmetrical relations, the past always forming the present without fully determining it. While the past is internal to the present, the present is (in part) external to the past. Thus time is a synthesis of the old and the new, the same and the different. The future, Hartshorne holds, does not consist of definite particular entities but of generalities or outlines, and the "future's becoming present" is the instantiation of these generalities or outlines. In short, temporal process is increase in concreteness, each event being partially self-creative. There are, of course, various levels of creativity in nature, ranging from the slightest flickers to conscious self-determination—and perhaps beyond. A normal human adult, because of his developed consciousness, is able to choose among *kinds* of acts, not merely among details of a single kind, and to do so on the basis of an embracing principle of value.[21]

---

20. See Hartshorne, "Causal Necessities," pp. 485-86.
21. See Hartshorne, *The Logic of Perfection*, p. 183.

Like Whitehead, Hartshorne employs the concept of a unit event or unit occasion—a quantum of concrete becoming. Compared with one another, the units differ in size or scope; some are brief, others extensive. A multiplicity of events may form a loose society or perhaps a holistic complex with as much unity as its best unified member events.[22] Each event brings novelty—if only a bit—into the world so that the order and monotony of things is always qualified by the zest of variety and the freshness of unpredictable contingency.

---

22. See Hartshorne, *Reality as Social Process*, p. 55.

5

NEOCLASSICAL THEISM

IN THE LENGTHY HISTORY OF WESTERN THOUGHT ABLE MINDS have repeatedly disagreed about the existence of God, some affirming, others denying, divine existence. Hartshorne, however, has sought to show that the question is not simply whether or not deity exists. Rather, the question is whether it is the existence of God or the non-existence of God that is without possible alternative—in short, whether divine existence is necessary or impossible. Hartshorne's argument is that the unsurpassable and worshipful being cannot be conceived in the mode of contingency, whether as existent or nonexistent. A creature by its very nature is contingent: it might not have existed in the first place, and will inevitably cease to exist. But were God to exist in this fashion, he would be surpassable (which is the same as saying he would not really be God at all), for a being whose existence is thus contingent and precarious is inferior to one who cannot fail to exist—and the same is true of a merely possible being, one that might exist though in fact it does not.

This assumes of course that the concept of a necessarily existing being makes sense. If it does not, then all beings are contingent, and deity, like unsurpassability, is impossible. But whether necessarily existing being is a legitimate concept or a piece of nonsense, both empirical theism—the doctrine that God exists but might not—and empirical atheism—the doctrine that God does not but might exist—are self-contradictory. In accordance with his metaphysical method, Hartshorne establishes the mode of God's existence by showing that contingency of divine existence (or of divine nonexistence) is incompatible with the concept of God, the denial of the noncontingency of God's existence being therefore meaningless. Once more, divine existence, while it must be noncontingent, may be either positively or negatively noncontingent. The real issue then is between a priori theism and positivism, the former affirming, the latter denying, the meaningfulness of theism. The question of God's existence, therefore, is not one of fact or observation but of meaning or logic.

Hartshorne has the distinction of having reopened discussion of the ontological argument, which since the time of Hume and Kant had been supposed a dead and closed issue. Critics have attacked Anselm's argument on various grounds, but most modern philosophers have accepted as decisive the Kantian criticism that Anselm makes existence a predicate. But is it an unexceptional rule that existence is not a predicate? Hartshorne points out that Kant's criticism, though it has force against one

—the earlier—form of Anselm's argument, is bootless against the stronger, modal form, which takes necessity of existence as a predicate.[1] If the existence as well as the nonexistence of a being are alike conceivable,[2] obviously the concept of that being will not provide a basis for inferring its existence; in short, existence will be no (deducible) predicate of the being. For example, we cannot tell whether a certain man exists simply from a definition or conception of the man. On the other hand, if the concept of a being, rather than permitting the alternative of its existing or not existing, instead excludes the possibility of its not existing, then necessity of existence is a deducible predicate of the being.[3] Kant's rule that existence is not a predicate may be generally true[4]—since contingency of existence is widespread!—but it cannot be universally true if the very conception of some being or other forbids its nonexistence. And, of

1. See Charles Hartshorne, "Introduction to Second Edition," *Saint Anselm: Basic Writings*, trans. S. N. Deane (La Salle, Ill.: Open Court Publishing Company, 1962), pp. 7–8; see also Hartshorne, "What Did Anselm Discover?" in *The Many-faced Argument*, ed. John H. Hick and Arthur C. Mc-Gill (New York: Macmillan Company, 1967), pp. 321–25; as well as Hartshorne, *Anselm's Discovery*, pp. 33–34.

2. See Hartshorne, *The Logic of Perfection*, p. 52, and his "What Did Anselm Discover?" p. 326.

3. See Charles Hartshorne, "The Formal Validity and Real Significance of the O n t o l o g i c a l Argument," *The Philosophical Review* 53, no. 3 (May 1944) : 227 and 233–34.

4. See Hartshorne, "Introduction," *Saint Anselm: Basic Writings*, pp. 7–8, and his *Anselm's Discovery*, p. 33.

course, what exists necessarily does exist,[5] existence in this case being a (deducible) predicate. Were anyone to argue that necessity of existence is not a predicate, he might be asked whether he intends to deny that modality of existence is a predicate.[6] If he admits (as the critics of the ontological argument do implicitly) that contingency of existence is a predicate, on what grounds can he deny that noncontingency of existence is a predicate?

Perhaps there is no being whose nature precludes its nonexistence. If not, it is because there *can* be no such being, since "a nonexistent being whose existence could be necessary" is nonsense.[7] On the other hand, if there can be such a being (one whose existence would be necessary), there must be.[8] The question then is whether we can legitimately conceive a being whose nonexistence is impossible. Anselm held that the concept of God—of that than which none greater can be conceived—is precisely the conception of one whose nonexistence is impossible, contingency of existence being surpassed by noncontingency of existence.[9] But is it true that a noncontingent being is one than which a greater is inconceivable? Anything that is wholly necessary is bereft of potentiality, hence is incapable of selecting among possibilities, and

----

5. See Hartshorne, *The Logic of Perfection*, p. 63.

6. See ibid., p. 52.

7. See ibid., p. 50 and p. 56; see also Hartshorne, "What Did Anselm Discover?" p. 322.

8. See Hartshorne, *The Logic of Perfection*, pp. 40, 53, 56, and 103; see also his "What Did Anselm Discover?" p. 327.

9. See Hartshorne, *Anselm's Discovery*, pp. 34–35.

seems therefore to be defective. For, as Hartshorne points out,[10] the power to select among possibilities is ordinarily taken as a measure of excellence, the greater the power (and the more the possibilities) the greater the excellence. But the Anselmian will reply that God is perfection, the unincreasable maximum of goodness, that if any possibility remained for him to realize he would be incomplete and thus imperfect. Hartshorne suggests that "the greatest possible value" may be no more sensible than "the greatest possible number," which is at best problematic.[11] One consideration here is that given values, were they actual, would make the realization of others impossible, since any actual state of affairs must be definitely *this*, not *that*, or else *that*, not *this*. Joint realization of all values is therefore impossible.[12] Another consideration is that possibility is in principle inexhaustible.[13] Indeed, only possibility can be strictly infinite, no possibility being exclusive of any other. But the compossibility of possibles, their compatibility and nonexclusiveness, betokens their status as determinables, in themselves indefinite and devoid of actual contrast, beauty, or value. Far from being the unincreasable full-

10. See Hartshorne, *The Logic of Perfection*, pp. 35–36.

11. See Hartshorne, *Anselm's Discovery*, p. 27; Hartshorne and Reese, *Philosophers Speak of God*, p. 103; and Hartshorne, "What Metaphysics Is," *The Journal of Karnatak University—Social Sciences* (Dharwar, India) 3 (1967): 12.

12. See Hartshorne, *Reality as Social Process*, p. 203, and his *The Logic of Perfection*, pp. 36, 37–38, and 42–43.

13. See Hartshorne, *Reality as Social Process*, p. 121.

ness of reality, the "absolutely infinite" turns out to be an abstraction, namely, the determinable features or aspects of reality.

To Anselm, God is unsurpassable only if changelessly complete. It appears that unless Anselm is mistaken in this, theism is in dire straits indeed. Is there any viable, alternative way to conceive the divine unsurpassability? God must be an actual being in order to be unsurpassable, and if actual he must somehow be finite, that is, determinate and restrictive of possibility. But surely a finite being can be surpassed. Not so, says Hartshorne, if by its very nature it includes all other beings, both actual and possible.[14] God as all-inclusive is unsurpassable though finite. Here the doctrine that God is finite means simply that God's all-inclusive actuality is a selection from the boundless possibles. A creature is not only finite but fragmentary as well; it is a part and only a part of the actual world. God is nonfragmentary because he includes all finite, fragmentary beings. But his inclusiveness is guaranteed only if he is capable of incorporating any and every change in reality, for failure to accommodate some new fact or other would render him surpassable, since a more inclusive and thus a greater being would then be conceivable. So the Unsurpassable must be infinitely flexible and adaptive, including in its actuality all actuality and in its potentiality whatever may be. Anselm, who assumed that even the atheist (the

14. See Hartshorne, *The Logic of Perfection*, pp. 34–40.

"fool") has a consistent idea of God, failed to see the absurdity in thinking that God, because he is strictly infinite, is therefore the fixed and unincreasable plenitude of being. If in order to make unsurpassability intelligible we must reject the implication of changelessness and say with Hartshorne that any possible thing would be God's actual possession were it actual at all,[15] then God can—indeed, he must—increase or grow in value and reality. Thus, divine "modal coincidence"—the doctrine that God's actuality is coextensive with all actuality and accordingly his potentiality with all possibility—appears snared in a dilemma. For if God increases he is not unsurpassable, and if unsurpassable he cannot increase.

Hartshorne has seen, however, that there is an ambiguity in the concept "unsurpassable." [16] A thing may be surpassable by another—or it may surpass itself. Anselm conceived God as surpassable neither by another nor by himself- as simply unsurpassable. We have seen that in order to surpass all others (actual or possible), God must be self-surpassing, for no other can rival him only if he everlastingly incorporates each new actualiza-

---

15. See Charles Hartshorne, "The Idea of God—Literal or Analogical?" *The Christian Scholar* 39, no. 2 (June 1956): 135–36.

16. See Hartshorne, *Man's Vision of God*, pp. 6–8; his *Reality as Social Process*, chap. 6, pp. 110–25; his "Introduction," *Saint Anselm: Basic Writings*, p. 6; his "What Did Anselm Discover?" p. 328; and his *The Logic of Perfection*, p. 35.

tion into himself. God may then be defined as the self-surpassing surpasser of all others.[17] Of course, his inclusion of any given state of the world is incomparable, as is his manner of self-surpassing or growth.

Hartshorne's understanding of deity—as that than which a greater *than itself* is inconceivable—seems consistent. Moreover, the all-important link between the concept of God and the modality of his existence becomes clearly visible on Hartshorne's view. God would not be modally infinite—in principle all-inclusive—were he capable of nonexistence, for in order to include all unfailingly he must exist and exist unconditionally. We are led then to ask whether divine all-inclusiveness makes sense. Here Hartshorne makes use of the age-old religious conviction that God is omniscient, that he knows without deficiency or distortion whatever there is to be known.[18] But to know something utterly is to possess or include it as a constituent.[19] God's all-inclusiveness is then a function of his perfect cognition. Such cognition, since it means participation in the concrete life of things, is also

17. See Charles Hartshorne, *The Divine Relativity: A Social Conception of God* (New Haven: Yale University Press, 1948), p. 20 and p. 60; see also his *Reality as Social Process*, p. 113.

18. See Hartshorne, *The Logic of Perfection*, pp. 37–38.

19. See Hartshorne, *The Divine Relativity*, pp. 64–65 and p. 69; see also Hartshorne and Reese, *Philosophers Speak of God*, p. 19; as well as Hartshorne, "The Structure of Givenness," *The Philosophical Forum* 18 (1960–61): 27 and 36; and Hartshorne, "The Dipolar Conception of Deity," *The Review of Metaphysics* 21, no. 2 (December 1967): 278.

perfect love. Far from being "impassible," God is supremely sensitive and relative to all. If God is nonfragmentary because of the universal scope of his relativity, does it follow that the whole content of the past and future is within that scope? He would surely be surpassable (since fragmentary) were he to omit any given item from the treasury of his knowledge. Hartshorne contends that the past is wholly retained in the divine memory, but that God possesses only vague outlines of the future[20]—not that he lacks what some conceivable being might have but that no concrete detail of the future is given, determinability being integral to futurity.

If God is sympathetically aware of whatever exists, he is influenced by the plethora of things he knows. Had these things been different in any way, God would correspondingly have been different. It follows that he is dependent or contingent on the objects of his knowledge, that is, on creatures. Can it be that God exists noncontingently because he is all-inclusive and is all-inclusive because he is contingent? This would indeed represent a reduction to absurdity for neoclassical theism were it a logical or theological requirement that God be either necessary or contingent but in no sense both. We have already seen that the doctrine of God as wholly necessary is nonsense, since he is unsurpassable (by others) only if

20. See Hartshorne, *Reality as Social Process*, p. 91, pp. 160–62, and p. 201, and Hartshorne and Reese, *Philosophers Speak of God*, pp. 93–96.

he is processive and relative. But the notion that God is wholly contingent is no less nonsensical. If there is any cogency in theism, it must then lie in a conception of God in which necessity and contingency are synthesized. One of Hartshorne's most brilliant contributions is his insight into this issue. He explains that in God there are two logical levels, one the abstract self-identity or individuality of God, the other the particular and concrete states of the divine life. These two levels are equivalent respectively to the existence and the actuality of God.[21] Just as I remain myself—that is, exist as a self —through a series of actual experiences, so does God. Not only is his godhood identically the same through the sequence of his various and different concretions, it cannot fail of exemplification in some divine concretion or other. For again, were nonexemplification possible, God would be surpassable, since contingently existent, and hence not God at all. Like a class that cannot be null, the divine essence must always be instantiated and therefore strictly necessary. On the other hand, the divine concretions, though they are each instances of the eternal essence of God, that is, instances of unsurpassability-by-another, are in themselves contingent totalities, any actuality being a selection from genuine alternatives. It is important to see that God-now is far more than that structure or essence which identifies deity as such and is

---

21. See Hartshorne, *The Logic of Perfection*, pp. 63–64, and his "What Did Anselm Discover?" p. 329.

definable a priori.[22] What the ontological argument proves if it is successful is that the divine essence is neither contingently exemplified nor contingently unexemplified, but it reveals absolutely nothing as to the concrete, detailed content of the divine life.[23]

We are now in a position to answer a troublesome question often raised with those who support the argument: how can anyone, beginning with a mere definition of something, deduce what is far richer in content, namely, its existence? Does not the argument purport to deduce the more from the less and succeed in pulling the rabbit from the hat only by sleight of hand? Hartshorne agrees thoroughly that there can be no logical descent from the abstract or general to the concrete, but he denies that the ontological argument (in neoclassical form) presumes to make that move.[24] The noncontingency of God's existence is an abstract property, the unexceptionable instantiation of perfection; it is no more concrete than the concept of perfection itself. A definition must be related to the concrete in one of the following logically possible ways: contingently exemplified, contingently unexemplified, necessarily exemplified, or necessarily unexemplified.[25] Each of these is an

---

22. See Hartshorne, *The Divine Relativity*, p. 31; *Reality as Social Process*, p. 176; *The Logic of Perfection*, p. 62 and p. 66.

23. See Hartshorne, "What Did Anselm Discover?" p. 329.

24. See ibid., as well as Hartshorne, *The Logic of Perfection*, pp. 46, 63, and 94.

25. See Hartshorne, *The Logic of Perfection*, p. 103.

abstract conception. The function of the ontological argument is to demonstrate the logical incompatibility between the concept of deity and the first and second in the list. Thus, the argument operates strictly by analysis of meanings and their connections. It can succeed as an a priori demonstration only because it does operate in this way. And only if it can succeed—and the question of divine existence can be removed from the sphere of contingency—does the argument escape the charge that it seeks to derive the concrete from the abstract. For were the argument incapable of succeeding, the existence of God would of necessity be contingent, and no logical argument could possibly establish it. The ontological argument would then be nonsense. What saves the argument, of course, is that the individuality of God (unlike that of any other being) is universal or nonparticular and may therefore be defined wholly by concepts, that is, a priori.[26] Any individual other than God is in some way limited or exclusive, but divine individuality (like every metaphysical principle) is implied by and embodied in any possible state of affairs.[27] That it cannot fail of exemplification is a property or predicate which follows analytically from the concept of divine individuality itself, and is indeed its (the concept's) unconditional universality. Neoclassical theism explains this universality by pointing out that whatever is or can be, is or can

26. See note 22 above.
27. See Hartshorne, *The Logic of Perfection*, p. 65.

be for God, God being unlimited in the scope and purity of his relativity to the ongoing creation.

With his classical conception of God, Anselm could not successfully have answered the charge of deducing the concrete. For him, God was absolutely simple, a unity without parts; hence, in seeking to deduce the divine existence Anselm was in truth seeking to deduce God in his totality. But the actual—of which Anselm (confusedly) thought God to be an absolutely unsurpassable maximum—is deducible from no definition.[28] Thus, in his argument, he was indeed pulling the rabbit from the hat. A being than which a greater is inconceivable cannot be a unity without parts, cannot be a purely necessary thing lacking any contingent features, and therefore cannot be exhaustively deduced from its conception. Perfection is not itself perfect.[29] If anything at all is, then perfection is its character or style or manner and consequently is an abstraction. Furthermore, if in the nature of the case this abstraction can never be unexemplified, it obtains necessarily. The necessity, however, does not attach to the concrete that exemplifies it. (If it did, the concrete would be surpassable by others, not perfect.) In order to make sense of the doctrine of God, we require the distinction between existential necessity and actual contingency, two logical levels within God himself, the one abstract, the other concrete. Far more serious than the assumption that existence is a predicate was Anselm's

---

28. See note 23 above.
29. See Hartshorne, *The Logic of Perfection*, pp. 52–53.

assumption that he had a consistent idea of God, and that even the atheist (the "fool") would admit its consistency. For without the above distinction between the existential and actual levels, Anselm's argument amounts to saying that perfection, were it capable of nonexistence, would be imperfect. There is of course no cogency in such reasoning, since the supposition that a predicate must be an instance of itself is fallacious.

Anselm's greatness is not dimmed by the fact that he worked within the context of classical theism. He could not have done otherwise, given his historical situation. As Hartshorne shows, Anselm's brilliant and original discovery concerning the divine existence can be clarified and strengthened when adapted for neoclassical theism, and this in itself is to Anselm's credit. The classical view of God, which for centuries was championed by learned men, has been found upon analysis to be incoherent. Were the classical view the only possible view of God, one would have to conclude with the positivists that God simply cannot exist. To argue that he exists necessarily would be like arguing that a round square exists necessarily.[30] Without a cogent and defensible idea of God, the ontological argument is impotent. The classical view is in trouble precisely because it insists that God, being changeless, does not interact with the world but remains impersonally independent of it. Of course, classical theologians asserted that God possesses personal characteristics such as love, knowledge, and will. But as Spinoza

30. See Hartshorne, "What Did Anselm Discover?" p. 327.

said with such incisiveness, to know or will anything contingent is insofar to be contingent—and of course the same goes for loving the contingent. If God is wholly noncontingent, it follows that he does not really love, know, or will the world, in which case he is far from perfect. Furthermore, if God is incapable of increase or growth, all talk about service to him is fatuous, since it is impossible to contribute anything to such a being.[31] The world itself would be of no use or value to him. He would be utterly indifferent and without concern for it, nor could he have any part in its creativity or its maintenance. The personalism of simple religious faith points the way out of such difficulties and provides the basis upon which a different, a neoclassical, conception of God can be built. Not only has Hartshorne systematized the conception of God as personal and relative; he has demonstrated its surprising capacity to do justice to the concerns of classical theism for the supremacy and permanence of God. Hartshorne's use of the neoclassical conception in connection with the ontological argument has made that argument formidable, and as a result the whole issue has been reopened for philosophical investigation and is being vigorously discussed.

It has been contended that all individual existents are contingent and that "a necessarily existent being" is therefore self-contradictory. The British philosopher J. N. Findlay employs such an argument in one of his

---

31. See Hartshorne, "The Dipolar Conception of Deity," p. 274.

articles.[32] He agrees that God, in order to satisfy religious claims and needs, would have to be one whose existence, like his excellence, no one could conceive away. Yet, Findlay argues, a necessary truth at most states the connection of certain characteristics, which may or may not have instances; it does not disclose whether there *will* be such instances. The religious man, therefore, demands that divine existence have the inescapability which belongs only to the connection of characteristics. He demands what cannot possibly be: an existent (that is, something contingent) that cannot not exist. Hartshorne, however, simply repudiates the dogma that all individual existence is contingent.[33] To be sure, all actuality is contingent. But existence is at a higher logical level than actuality and possesses a certain independence from it. If (though only if) existence is in some exceptional case wholly nonselective or nonrestrictive of possibilities, it is indeed inescapable. And, of course, in neoclassical theism God is modally all-inclusive, and therefore his existence excludes no possible state of affairs.

Were God, merely by existing, to exclude an otherwise possible state of affairs, his existence would be

---

32. Findlay's article, "Can God's Existence Be Disproved?" is reprinted in *The Ontological Argument from St. Anselm to Contemporary Philosophers*, ed. Alvin Plantinga (Garden City, N.Y.: Doubleday & Company, 1965), pp. 111–21. See particularly pp. 119–20.

33. See Hartshorne, "Structure of Metaphysics," p. 230; his *The Logic of Perfection*, pp. 30–31; and his "Negative Facts and the Analogical Inference to 'Other Mind,'" p. 149.

empirical and contingent. Creatures exist thanks only to the fact that certain possibilities have not been actualized, and this distinguishes them categorically from the deity. From the conception or definition of a creature, the only necessary truth that can be drawn respecting its existence is that that existence is contingent. Accordingly, knowledge as to whether it does in fact exist must be a posteriori, empirical. The existence of God, being categorically different, must be known in a categorically different—namely, an a priori—way. It follows, as Hartshorne insists, that there can be no empirical proofs of divine existence.[34] This does not mean that the only proof is the ontological proof but that every proof must, like the ontological proof, be nonempirical. For example, an argument from design must not involve the assumption that God can exist only if such and such orderly conditions prevail. For this implies that God's existence is factual, that it could be falsified by the negative evidence that the required conditions were absent. The argument must instead demonstrate that any possible world requires order and that only a cosmic individual can provide it. Here we have a question of meanings, not of fact, and if the argument is successful the existence of a divine orderer is shown to be without rational alternative. According to Hartshorne, the other arguments

---

34. See Charles Hartshorne, "Religious Aspects of Necessity and Contingency," in *Great Issues Concerning Theism*, ed. Charles H. Monson, Jr. (Salt Lake City: University of Utah Press, 1965), p. 147.

for divine existence must fit the same pattern and demonstrate the incoherence of attempts to construe divine existence as nonnecessary. If so, each can be taken as an illustration of Hartshorne's method, whereby metaphysical truth is established by the reduction of its denial to absurdity.

Hartshorne holds that although God orders the world, he does not regulate it down to the last detail.[35] In other words, the world is not just a result of divine action; every individual acts and is to some degree responsible for producing the world that is produced. God sets limits to the chaos and disorder which inevitably accompany the actions of a multiplicity of agents. He treasures their creativity and incorporates their creations in his own life. The ultimate purpose of a creature is to enrich itself and the world about it in order thereby to add some bit of beauty or value to the immortal God, who everlastingly surpasses himself, but to whom no other can compare.

---

35. See Hartshorne, *The Divine Relativity*, p. 136, and his *Reality as Social Process*, pp. 190–92.

6

THE HARTSHORNIAN ECONOMY

THE READER WILL PERHAPS HAVE REALIZED THAT MATERIAL-ism, determinism, and atheism may each be seen as a denial of a corresponding conjunction, the rejection of one, though only one, of its conjuncts. Each of the three alternatives is a sort of *tollendo ponens*, its apparent positivity being in truth all that remains after pure negation of one pole of a contrast. Materialism denies sentient-and-extended, determinism free-and-caused, and atheism contingent-and-necessary. The neoclassical strategy is to reveal the negativity and incoherence of each denial and thereby establish in each case a "both-and." It is in this sense that we can understand Hartshorne's claim that neoclassical metaphysics represents a novel "higher synthesis." [1] It says of any given category: "This, yes, but not only this—nor only its contrary—but this as well as its contrary." The key, of course, is that a category and its contrary represent two logically different levels of

---

1. See Hartshorne, *Reality as Social Process,* p. 18, and Hartshorne and Reese, *Philosophers Speak of God,* p. 512.

reality, the one concrete, the other abstract. The togetherness of the two levels is merely the togetherness of concrete and abstract, one category representing the fullness
of reality, the other only features, aspects, or relations of
it. Hence, the relationship between the two levels is
that of whole to part, so that one of two contrasting categories is always inclusive of the other. Another way to
conceive the relationship is to think of it as constituting
a mean between extremes, between a category and its
contrary, each taken to the exclusion of the other.

Materialism and determinism deny neoclassical doctrine by excluding the concreteness of things. Materialism leaves only the extended, determinism the caused.
Atheism denies neoclassical doctrine by excluding the
abstract character of deity, leaving only contingency. But
just as there are many ways of missing a target, so there
are many ways of missing philosophical truth. Thus, not
only have there been materialists; there have also been
those who repudiated extension altogether, for example,
illusionistic monists like Sankara and F. H. Bradley.
And not only have there been absolute determinists but
absolute indeterminists as well, Jean-Paul Sartre perhaps
being a contemporary example of the latter.[2] Moreover,
classical theism (of which Aquinas is the supreme repre-
sentative) is a position exactly contrary to atheism, the
classical position being that God is wholly without con-

---

2. Sartre does not, of course, deny causality in nature,
apart from man.

tingency. The alternatives, some of them overshooting the neoclassical "higher synthesis," others undershooting it, are a numerous congeries distracting attention from that synthesis itself and from its internal coherence. What should not be overlooked is that the synthesis not only brings each category into union with its contrary but also each categorial contrast into union with all the others. The principle of asymmetry by which any of the categories is related to its contrary is the same as that by which every other is related to its contrary. The union of categorial contrasts, however, is not merely analogical. It is literal. For there is an equivalence among the categories expressing the abstract as there is among those expressing the concrete. Accordingly, each categorial contrast is a variation on the same metaphysical theme— that being is within becoming. The relation between being and becoming cannot of course be symmetrical. Nor can becoming be part of being. Rather, becoming is the inclusive reality, being its included component.

One way of describing Hartshorne's metaphysics is to call it dipolar. It illustrates what Morris Cohen has spoken of as the "Law of Polarity," the law that ultimate contraries *taken conceptually* are correlative and mutually interdependent.[3] There is a remarkable economy in dipolar metaphysics. For principles that have been conceived as distinct and competitive—some have even

---

3. See Hartshorne, *Reality as Social Process,* p. 86; Hartshorne and Reese, *Philosophers Speak of God,* p. 2; and his "Ontological Argument," p. 231.

said the principles were in tension or conflict with one another—are brought into harmony, apparent incompatibility being reduced to contrast within unity. In truth, the economy afforded by neoclassical metaphysics requires fewer ultimates than do classical systems. This is true because the concrete is inclusive of the abstract and hence explains it, the converse relation being impossible. Thus, the dipolar "higher synthesis" is no democracy of categories, no confederation *inter pares*. Without making an invidious comparison between poles of a categorial contrast, dipolar metaphysics nonetheless relates the poles asymmetrically—in the whole-part relationship—and in this sense subordinates one pole to the other. Since the term *economy* connotes organization or system as well as thrift, we may say that neoclassical metaphysics gains efficiency (is in the latter sense economical) by its dipolar economy (former sense of the term).

Is the Hartshornian economy reductionistic? Of course, it reduces the number of "ultimates." Indeed, there is in the final analysis but one ultimate: creativity. But does not the Hartshornian economy dissolve the many into the one, reducing everything to reality-as-process? Once more, dipolarity is the preservation of the polar distinctions, not their abrogation. It negates nothing except nonsense—in accordance with the axiom that a metaphysical truth is wholly positive. Moreover, it elucidates the relationship between the poles of a fundamental contrast, putting the one into context with the other. Do we really illuminate that relationship when we rely merely on the symmetrical "and"—this pole *and* its contrary? How does that help? It may of course keep us from taking sides between ultimate contraries and either reducing the one to the other or simply "cleaving to the one and denying the other." But while elaboration of the categorial themes is part of the philosophical program, it is not the whole of it. Plato elaborated those themes as well as any philosopher in Western history, but he failed to explain satisfactorily how they exist together in consistency.[4] Flux and forms, yes, but how much light is shed by saying that the flux "participates" in the forms? Far less light, if any at all, is shed on the relation by a mere "and." Paul Tillich speaks of "dynamics and form" as one of the ontological polarities; yet the conjunction scarcely explains the togetherness of the two poles, and to make matters worse Tillich wanders off into mythological language about their separation or alienation from each other.

The crucial question is whether one pole of every categorial contrast *can* be construed as designating a level of reality within the whole, the other pole designating the whole itself. If philosophers have treated the members of a polar contrast on a parity with one another logically and metaphysically, or else denied one of the pair or subordinated the wrong one (the concrete), it seems that many find it far from obvious that one mem-

---

4. See Hartshorne and Reese, *Philosophers Speak of God*, p. 40.

ber of each pair expresses only an aspect or constituent of the concrete. Is the permanent a part of the changing, the absolute a part of the relative, the potential a part of the actual, and so forth? Obviously, the question can be ramified indefinitely, each addition being but a variation on the theme. Rather than taking first the theme, let us look at a number of the variations.

To begin, consider the subject-object structure. A subject, taken concretely, is a self-active experience, a unit which may endure for only a fraction of a second. The subject-object structure, therefore, is really the experience-object structure. As we pointed out in a previous discussion, experience is essentially relational. It is senseless to talk about experience that is not "of" something experienced. Nor can an experience have itself as an object.[5] "Experience of" is always "experience of another." Yet, the other that is experienced is not relativized by being experienced: it is externally related to the subject experiencing it. Indeed, the object is antecedent (albeit slightly) to the subject and independent of it. But the subject is dependent upon the object it experiences, being internally related to that object. The subject-object relation is, therefore, asymmetrical, for while the object is part of the subject-experience, the subject-experience is not part of the object. The object's being a constituent of the experience of it is not, of course, a datum of that very

5. See Hartshorne, "The Structure of Givenness," pp. 23, 34, 36–37, as well as his *The Logic of Perfection*, p. 227.

experience but only of some subsequent experience, since no experience has itself as object.

The striking thing is that experience is essentially outreaching or, to use Whitehead's term, prehensive. It seizes the object per se, not merely an idea or impression of the object.[6] Kant's theory of "appearances" or "phenomena" assumes that the knowing of an object is really only the knowing of the *knowing* of the object.[7] But if an experience is never its own object, Kant is surely mistaken; moreover, his theory initiates a needless—and vicious—regress. Hartshorne has at times explained the prehensive character of experience by saying that awareness is always a form of memory, either personal (introspective) or impersonal (sensory—unless telepathic or mystical). Note that on this interpretation all introspection is retrospection.[8]

Moreover, if experience of an object is an asymmetrical relation, internal one way and external the other, then Hume (or Russell) is mistaken and so is Bradley, but in opposite ways.[9] It is false that all relatedness is external, just as it is false that all relatedness is internal. In either case we have an instance of "monopolar" philosophizing, Hume and Russell opting for the absolute to the exclusion of the relative, Bradley for the relative to the exclusion of the absolute. The

---

6. See Hartshorne, "The Structure of Givenness," p. 25.
7. See Unpublished Manuscript, p. 37.
8. See Hartshorne, "The Structure of Givenness," p. 37.
9. See ibid., p. 25.

dipolar view, of course, incorporates both absoluteness (with respect to the object) and relatedness (with respect to the subject). The object, then, is a nonrelative part of the subject. The subject is therefore a concrete whole inclusive of the object, while the object is an abstractable constituent of that whole.

It is improper to conceive a subject as a fully-formed entity that in addition has a relation to some object. Relation to an object is constitutive of the subject and inseparable from it. A different object means a different subject—even though the difference may be slight. "For example, remembering past pleasure is a different sort of experience from remembering past pain."[10] An object then is a cause of its subject. Therefore, in turning to the cause-effect relation, we really continue to discuss the object-subject relation. For, as Hartshorne remarks, "to explain how something influences an experience, we have only to explain how this something comes to be an object or content of the experience."[11] "Causation" is here taken to mean that one thing (the effect) logically *requires* another (the cause), not, as with Hume, that the effect merely follows the cause.[12] Since the effect entails the cause, it is inseparable from it. Asymmetrically, the cause is separable from the effect, independent of it. Hume's dictum, that the distinguishable is separable, works one way only: for the object with respect to

10. Hartshorne, *The Logic of Perfection*, p. 227.
11. Ibid.
12. See Hartshorne, "The Structure of Givenness," p. 25.

the subject, but not vice versa. Still, the effect—or subject-experience—is not just the cause—or object—all over again without addition. Experience of X includes X—and more. The "more" is the definiteness of feeling and evaluation regarding X. This feeling and evaluation is certainly not supplied by X itself. Rather, it is emergent, the subject being partially self-creative. Causation, then, is not total determination, and every subject-experience is therefore a composite of freedom and limitation, a synthesis of the new and the old.

But how can the object-subject or cause-effect relation constitute a gain in definiteness? Are objects or causes indefinite? Of course, if they are universals, there is no reason to doubt their indefiniteness. The number "two," for example, is indefinite.[13] Two what? Two days, two fish, two ideas, two men? Whenever the number is instantiated, in things or in our thought and experience, it is given a context of concrete detail. Its instantiation—one is tempted to say its incarnation—is the resolution of its indeterminateness by a factual situation. Hartshorne, however, conceives *every* experience as a gain in definiteness, not just the experience of universals. Take the case of a man thinking about the events of the day as he retires to bed. Certainly he can add

13. See Charles Hartshorne, "Santayana's Doctrine of Essence," in *The Philosophy of George Santayana*, ed. Paul A. Schilpp (Evanston, Ill.: Northwestern University, 1940), pp. 163–64; his *The Divine Relativity*, pp. 62–63; and his "What Metaphysics Is," p. 3.

nothing to the events themselves, any more than he can subtract from them. Yet, "thinking of those events" is a kind of universal, capable of being instantiated in an indefinite number of ways. And the man in his night-shirt instantiates that universal in one definite and detailed way. Every actuality *is* definite and detailed, but its future is not; and it is precisely this future which is being settled as the actuality becomes object for subsequent actualities. As Whitehead put it, "it belongs to the nature of a 'being' that it is a potential for every [subsequent] 'becoming'."[14] An entity, though actual in and of itself, is nonetheless potential for other, subsequent, actualities. This explains why experience of the past is always gain in definiteness: it is the actualization of that potentiality which, for the past, constitutes the future.

A subject's anticipation of future actualization, or its purposing, is a form of the subject-object relation. In this case, however, the subject directs itself not to given actuality (the past) but to potential actuality (the future). Thus, anticipation-fulfillment is the relation of subject to subsequent object. Of course, the subject does not experience actualities belonging to its future. It may intend them or wish them or fear them, but in no case does it experience them. There are no such actualities for it to experience; they are all yet to be. Even if

---

14. Alfred North Whitehead, *Process and Reality: An Essay in Cosmology* (New York: Macmillan Co., 1929), p. 33.

predicted, they are nonetheless not *there* to be experienced. For prediction gives us only an outline and, as Hartshorne points out, "it is an outline qualifying the past, a direction in which events have already been tending."[15] All looking forward, all anticipation, is tinctured with indefiniteness, not the indefiniteness of pure possibility but of real or restricted possibility. Real possibility constitutes a class of alternatives, a class of which whatever actuality eventuates from that possibility will be a member. "But within the class, or in so far as the proximate potentiality is less sharply definite than actuality, there are limits within which the event decides for itself." [16] Hence, real possibility is a kind of universal, a relatively limited universal, but nonetheless a universal, as innocent of the precise quality of its member-events-yet-to-be as of their actuality. Indeed, precise or particular quality *is* actuality.[17]

Real possibility is futurity, and the resolution of its ambiguity is achieved by creation of new definiteness. We call this process of actualization the present. Time, then, is cumulative in definiteness, hence, asymmetrically structured. The emergence of novelty is the very meaning of occurrence. To be sure, "every event is caused, that is to say, it issues out of a restricted or real potentiality; but also, every event occurs by chance, that is

---

15. Hartshorne, "The Structure of Givenness," p. 26.
16. Hartshorne, *Reality as Social Process*, p. 89.
17. See ibid., p. 98.

to say, it is more determinate than its proximate real potentiality, and just to that extent is unpredictable, undeducible from its causes and causal laws." [18] Thus, the cause-effect relation coincides with the past-present relation. Hartshorne holds that time, far from being a "fourth dimension of space," is the more fundamental order.[19] Indeed, space is to be explained as a certain complexity in the temporal or causal structure. We are influenced by our ancestors but not they by us; we will influence our remote descendents, but not they us. The dependence is entirely one-way, the reason being simply that there can be interaction only among neighbors. To have a neighbor is to coexist with another. Of course, events that coexist as contemporaries are mutually independent, and one of them can no more be the cause of another than it can be prior or posterior to another. Hence, the coexistence of interactive neighbors is the coexistence of temporal sequences, that is, of enduring individuals. The mutual dependence of two such individuals is really an abstraction from the basic temporal relation of events. For one concrete event, in order to effect another, must be prior to it. If the two events belong to different sequences, the effected (later) event may in turn influence events in the other sequence—but only those subsequent to it. To speak of reciprocity

18. Ibid., pp. 88–89.
19. See Hartshorne, "The Structure of Givenness," pp. 29–30, as well as Unpublished Manuscript, p. 40.

between individuals is therefore to gloss over the asymmetry of the relation between one concrete momentary experience and another.

Space or extension, then, is the order of mutuality, mutual independence in the case of contemporary events, mutual dependence in the case of enduring individuals.[20] We have at this point returned to the doctrine that extension is an abstraction from the concrete. There is on Hartshorne's interpretation no need to posit "mere matter" to account for space. Since temporal relations are always unidirectional, mutuality must be explained by some order distinguishable from time. Abstracting from the concrete momentary experiences in a sequence, we can identify an enduring *gen-identity*—the person or thing that can exchange influences with other persons or things. Or, abstracting from concrete momentary experiences, all of them contemporary with one another, we are left with a spatial expanse—the "matter" disclosed in sensory experience.

Just as matter is an appearance of the concrete (a phenomenal simplification of the coexistence of events), so too with cause. It is the appearance of the already created from the perspective of the now creating. In Hartshorne's aphorism, "Causality is crystallized freedom, freedom is causality in the making." [21] No separate principle of causality is required—only subjects, which

20. See Hartshorne, "The Structure of Givenness," p. 30.
21. Hartshorne, *The Logic of Perfection*, p. 233.

from the perspective of subsequent subjects are objects, and hence causes. Once more, the Hartshornian economy is in evidence.

In general, all of these structures coincide. They are, as we said, variations on a theme, and that theme can be expressed in categorial form: the abstract is within the concrete, the absolute within the relative. To put the theme more concretely, though somewhat cryptically, we may say that time is objective modality. Peirce said that time is "a species of objective modality." [22] Hartshorne prefers the simpler formulation. For time, viewed concretely, is the cumulation of novel actuality, event by event. It contains positive contingency (past actuality) as well as negative (the future). And the latter includes not only the indefinite fecundity of pure, logical possibility but also the restriction of that fecundity (by the actual course of things) to a range of alternatives, or real possibilities, from which the next phase of actualization must issue. Moreover, necessity, being that in which possibilities agree, is also implicit in time. Unconditional necessity is the highly abstract factor common to all possibilities whatsoever, whereas conditional necessity is the more concrete factor common to a set of real possibilities.[23] Note that the invariant or eternal is a function of time.[24] Until Bergson and Whitehead, philosophers

---

22. See Hartshorne and Reese, *Philosophers Speak of God*, p. 11, and Hartshorne, "What Metaphysics Is," p. 4.

23. See Hartshorne, *Reality as Social Process*, p. 86.

24. See Hartshorne, "What Metaphysics Is," p. 5.

almost always put it the other way around and tried to explain becoming in terms of being.[25] Hartshorne, in consonance with those two thinkers, has seen that reality *is* social, creative process, "the concrete from which alone any abstractions can be abstracted." [26]

The Hartshornian economy, with its coincidence of the various polarities and synthesis of each polar pair, is exemplified in eminent form in God. Time, we may say, has its ideal exemplar—the divine being. Far from being the purely unconditioned, the *ens necessarium*, of classical theology, God is here viewed as the incomparable subject (or subject-sequence), the world being his object. Thus, the subject-object structure finds its supreme illustration in God's relation to the world. Abstract from God's present experience and you get the world immediately past—and its antecedents. Abstract from the sequence of divine states and you get God's essence, that is, his defining character identifying him as an individual. God literally instantiates the categories: "He is the literal instance (because the original one) of the categories; they are himself in his individual essence." [27] By contrast, other subjects, the creatures, only instantiate the categories with qualifications, the application of those concepts being analogical—rather than univocal, as is the case with deity. Hence, "God is the

---

25. See ibid., p. 2.
26. Ibid., p. 5.
27. Hartshorne, *The Divine Relativity*, p. 36.

one individual conceivable a priori." [28] This, of course, follows from his being the subject whose relativity to objects is without deficiency. For if the categories or polar contraries merely formulate the subject-object relation in more abstract terms, they will be exhibited in all instances of that relation, and ideally so in the case of the unsurpassable subject. Classical theism said in effect that God is not a subject at all, but a mere object. He could be experienced but could not experience. The (unseen) implication was that the-world-plus-God is greater than God alone! [29] To be sure, God is an object for creatures and is therefore included by them. But not *simpliciter*. For creaturely intuitions of God are at best faint and ineffective,[30] whereas his intuitions of creatures are pure and completely adequate. Hence, God "unqualifiedly or with full effectiveness has or contains us," [31] and accordingly we are abstractions from his concrete fullness. The unity of being—to use the title of Hartshorne's doctoral dissertation—is the unity of object in subject, cause in effect, past in present, the world in God being the eminent form of each.

---

28. Ibid., p. 31.
29. See ibid., p. 19.
30. See ibid., p. 92.
31. Ibid.

THE AESTHETIC MOTIF

«««««««««««««««««««««««

HARTSHORNE REMARKS THAT THE AESTHETIC PROBLEM is basically the same as the metaphysical problem.[1] The connection he sees between aesthetics and metaphysics is suggested by his conception of metaphysics as a synthesis of the fundamental contraries, the synthesis representing a mean between contrary extremes. Being a synthesis of the contraries, that mean is not to be construed as something intermediate between the extremes—as gray is intermediate between red and green—but as a composite of both. Accordingly, metaphysics is to exhibit the principle of aesthetic harmony, the principle of unity in variety. Without unity, there is chaos and confusion; without variety, deadly order and monotony.[2]

But how is the metaphysician to avoid one or the other of the aesthetic evils—discord or insipidity—without coming to rest at some dull gray-point between them?

---

1. See Hartshorne, *Man's Vision of God*, p. 220.
2. See ibid., pp. 212–13; see also Hartshorne, *Reality as Social Process*, p. 46; "The Aesthetics of Birdsong," *The Journal of Aesthetics and Art Criticism* 26, no. 3 (Spring 1968): 311.

If likeness and difference were univocal or unidimensional, being end points respectively of a single continuum, there could be no satisfactory reply, only an admission of the predicament. But there are various *respects* in which things are alike or diverse,[3] and therefore unity and variety can increase together, though in different respects or dimensions. "You can add to the variety of colors, while increasing the similarity of shapes, or vice versa."[4] Moreover, color, like shape, is itself multidimensional. To stick with our example, red and green contrast sharply with one another, but at the same time they are similar in a number of ways. Both are colors, they may be of equal "saturation" and "brightness," and so forth.[5] Indeed, so complex is the multidimensionality of existence that it defies complete analysis. However, by confining attention to the categorial dimensions of existence, one can abstract from the complexity of particular qualities or special structures, and by virtue of this simplification produce an aesthetic metaphysics.

There can be little doubt as to the aesthetic inspiration guiding Hartshorne's neoclassical thinking. How but by aesthetic sensitivity can one penetrate to the concrete? And how save by such penetration can one develop metaphysics, which is the theory of concreteness? Philosophy, according to Whitehead, is "the critic of ab-

---

3. See Hartshorne, *Reality as Social Process*, p. 46.
4. Hartshorne, *Man's Vision of God*, p. 213.
5. See Hartshorne, *Reality as Social Process*, pp. 45–46.

stractions," but as Hartshorne explains,[6] the abstractions are criticized not because they conflict with the facts but because they stand in need of supplementation by other abstractions and are insofar deficient as an account of the meaning of concreteness. Science, for example, is to be criticized because it abstracts from value or quality. It leaves these aside in order to focus on what can be publicly observed and mathematically expressed. The procedure is legitimate and reasonable, but it entails disregard of principles, not just of details. "In all human knowing there must be abstraction, disregarding of details, but it is one thing to disregard details and another to disregard aspects quite as universal as those taken into account." [7] From "concreteness" *only* details are omitted —not principles, however unmanageable they may be.

Is value or quality really a universal principle? Not if ethical value or quality is meant, for value is sought and enjoyed by subethical creatures, by infants and non-human animals, for example.[8] But if aesthetic value is meant, then the answer is that value is not only universal but in truth the clue to all else. Every unit-event realizes some immediate (aesthetic) value and in turn is of value to unit-events that experience it. Thinking and perceiving are both modes of valuing, as Hartshorne points

6. See Hartshorne, "What Metaphysics Is," p. 3.
7. Ibid.
8. See Hartshorne, *Reality as Social Process*, p. 44.

out.[9] They involve taking an interest, being attracted by and attentive to something that has value, however slight. It is often said that sensation arouses emotion, and there is no good reason to deny this. But Hartshorne contends that some of the feeling "connected with" one's sensations simply *is* the sensations![10] In other words, a color, sound, odor, or taste is itself a feeling tone, a "localized emotion" in contrast to other, diffused emotions and feelings. Consider the complementary colors. "Red is felt in artistic appreciation as warm, insistent, advancing; its bluish-green complementary is cool, gentle, receding. Yellow is lively, cheerful, light-hearted; blue-violet is quiet, wistful, earnest." [11] Moreover, the sense qualities of one sense organ are not without affinity for those of the other sense organs. Simple colors, sounds, odors, tastes, pressures, and pains all belong on an affective continuum,[12] each representing an island of feeling not really disconnected from the others.

The usual mind-set of modern men living in technological society is pragmatic, not aesthetic. To be sure, "nothing can be valued wholly for itself, not even the dearest of friends, nor yet wholly as a means, not even a

---

9. See Charles Hartshorne, *The Philosophy and Psychology of Sensation* (Chicago: University of Chicago Press, 1934), p. 163; his *Man's Vision of God*, p. 223; his "What Metaphysics Is," p. 4; and Unpublished Manuscript, p. 86.

10. See Hartshorne, *The Philosophy and Psychology of Sensation*, p. 180.

11. Ibid., p. 165.

12. See ibid., p. 5 ff.

brass tack." [13] But the emphasis is different where the pragmatic attitude dominates. Sensation is used rather than enjoyed. It functions as a sign to be read ("green means go," "at the sound of the tone, it will be twelve-thirty," "it smells as if something's burning"). The child, the primitive man, and the artist, being less obsessed with practical and intellectual concerns, find the world more vivid and absorbing. They enter naïvely into the great "ocean of feelings," in whose aesthetic richness each experience participates. But most of us select out aspects of experience, primarily its nonparticipatory features (those which require of us little or no feeling involvement), for attention and use. We are thus left with a pragmatic skeleton of concrete experience. As Hartshorne observes, we fail to realize that there is a prosaic fallacy, not just a pathetic fallacy, for we suppose that what bankers, farmers, engineers, businessmen, and scientists need not attend to is unimportant or absent.[14] If awareness of the concrete is always aesthetic—a feeling of quality—then, of course, practical and intellectual knowledge is secondary. It is appropriation of things by abstraction. And when we mistake our abstractions for the concrete, we are indeed in the grip of the prosaic fallacy and thus are misled in our description of experience. "The world is not so tame as prosy people are apt to suppose." [15]

---

13. Ibid., p. 187.
14. See Unpublished Manuscript, pp. 85–86.
15. Ibid., p. 86.

Aesthetic value is intrinsic or immediate. And nothing possesses such value more fully than living feeling and emotion. "The attempt to interpret the aesthetic datum as at once intrinsically beloved and yet (as given) not intrinsically alive and emotional—that is to say, genuinely lovable—is the fundamental contradiction of modern aesthetics." [16] In Hartshorne's panpsychic, social conception of reality each experient-event is an aesthetic fulfillment and hence an end in itself. Yet, it is also a means to the aesthetic fulfillment of other, subsequent experient-events. For an experient-event is always a datum, a gift to the future, and experient-events yet to be will arise by receiving such data and fusing their (the data's) aesthetic attainments into further aesthetic attainments. Thus, sentience is no less the secret of the enjoyed than of enjoyment itself.

The genius of the social, panpsychic view is that it furnishes insight into the structure of reality as essentially aesthetic, a structure of unity in variety. From the ultramicroscopic level up, there is integration of variety into organic wholeness. An electron is an instance of such integration on a relatively small scale, an atom on a somewhat larger scale, the contrasts unified within the atom being greater.[17] We can move from these elementary unities to molecules and cells and from these upward until we reach the higher types of being. Here

16. Hartshorne, *The Philosophy and Psychology of Sensation*, p. 168.
17. See Hartshorne, *Man's Vision of God*, p. 216.

too the aesthetic structure is illustrated. Thus, an animal is the unity of its bodily region and of the variety therein. But how is the oneness of the many to be understood? Certainly, the many cannot be one at the same time and in the same respect that they are many. However, they can in some *other* respect be one. There are, as Hartshorne says, "respects" of comparison.[18] The polarity of self and other gives us two levels of analysis, hence, two "respects" of comparison. We return, then, to the idea of multidimensionality, which, as we have indicated, is so basic to aesthetic interpretation. But now we are interested in viewing that idea in the context of social-temporal relatedness. Fundamentally, social feeling is "feeling of feeling." [19] In our concrete experience there is always "a direct grasp of life fusing into other life, of end-in-itself in one with our end." [20]

Hartshorne remarks that social harmony-in-contrast is superior to other forms of harmony in that one side of the contrast also appears (more or less completely) on the other side. Thus, it is not that a subject and its object are unified by some third thing; rather, they are unified by the subject, which includes the object as a constituent. In spite of its inclusion of its object—or, really, because of that inclusion—the subject is nonidentical with the object and in contrast to it. The unity

18. See Hartshorne, *Reality as Social Process*, p. 46.
19. See Hartshorne, *The Philosophy and Psychology of Sensation*, p. 193.
20. Ibid., p. 187.

is strictly from the side of the subject, since the subject is not the object's datum and therefore is not a constituent part of the object's unity. This of course implies that the variety is also strictly from the side of the subject, the subject's contrast with the object representing no real fact about the object in its concreteness. By "subject" as also by "object" we mean here a unit-event, not an enduring individual. Asymmetrical unity in variety is precisely the aesthetic pattern we might have expected, given our analysis of the one-way relatedness of unit-events.

Since the concrete is the inclusive form of reality, "from which alone any abstractions can be abstracted,"[21] an object may be said to be abstract with respect to the subject including it. The object in itself is, of course, fully determinate, but "relation to it" is not settled by the object itself but by the subject which has it as object. But this is merely to say that becoming is cumulative or additive in concreteness. Abstracting from creative process, one is left with aspects of the concrete—with its character, pattern, or structure—and to these the name "abstract" applies without qualification. Sensory experience involves a form of abstraction from the concrete, one that is usually unwitting. The sensory character is separated from the sensory quality and is taken (or, better, mistaken) for the concrete sensory experience itself. Then it is claimed that feeling is

---

21. Hartshorne, "What Metaphysics Is," p. 5.

somehow "associated with" the sensory character. But in vivid, aesthetic observation feelings are not experienced merely as together with sensations but rather as inhering in them.[22] Says Hartshorne: "Philosophers need to cultivate the capacity to see experience generally (not just works of art) artistically, or as artists, poets, primitive men, and children see it, so that they can put the abstract back into the setting in which it belongs." [23] Put in its setting, the abstract furnishes an aesthetic contrast with the concrete, again in asymmetrical unity-in-variety. Not only is the abstract experienced aesthetically as a general presence within the concrete but also, at a higher level, as possibility haunting the actual. The contrast between what may be and what is, and between what might have been and what is, a contrast which in each case belongs to what is, lends poignancy and intensity to experience. In the one direction is regret or relief; in the other, fear or expectancy.

A categorial scheme is only a general –indeed, the most general—formulation of the unity of things. It must reflect the fundamental harmony of reality, though it may interpret that harmony in a logical rather than an aesthetic context.[24] Hence, such a scheme may fall into imbalance, not just into incoherence. For too much likeness will yield triviality, and too much difference,

22. See Hartshorne, *The Philosophy and Psychology of Sensation,* p. 174.
23. Unpublished Manuscript, p. 88.
24. See Hartshorne, *Man's Vision of God,* p. 220.

discord. "We say that variety is the spice of life, but we know equally well that spice by itself is not a satisfying diet." [25]

Consider the extremes. On the one hand is unity without variety, on the other variety without unity. Philosophers have at times described the world as a pure unity or spoken of God as simple, that is, without part. But aside from the question as to whether such utterances make sense, there is the question as to whether they refer to anything of value. It is false that beauty is in the eye of the beholder; yet there could be no beauty or, more generally, no value without the eye of the beholder, nor without something beheld. For value involves awareness, and awareness the duality of subject and object—hence, variety. And there are other considerations which lead to the conclusion that pure unity would be valueless.[26] One is that a state without variety would not only lack any contrast between degrees or levels of actual value but also between actual and possible value. But an actuality is always a selection from possibility, and therefore its value must be contrasted with alternative values.[27] Without actuality, there is nothing at all. Therefore, if there is something (and there must be), there is the contrast between the possible and the actual—hence, variety.

---

25. Ibid., p. 212.
26. See ibid.
27. See ibid.

Would variety without unity represent anything of value? Surely a thing of value, however humble, is no mere aggregate. Moreover, even the coarsest aggregate is not without unity. For example, its parts must be units of some sort. Otherwise, of what would it be the aggregate? And, of course, in speaking of "the aggregate," we suggest an identifiable plurality and thus a togetherness of parts—hence, unity. To be sure, the unity of the aggregate may be very loose indeed. There may be conflict among its parts, so that the aesthetic value of the aggregate is slight. Yet conflict is out of the question where *(per impossible)* the parts have absolutely nothing in common. In such a hypothetical state monads would truly be windowless. One could be neither valuable nor even interesting to another. Accordingly, value would have to attach to each monad simply in and of itself. But how, if each is an unqualified manyness? For without unity, there is no experience (nor so much as *a* thing at all). But value requires experience—hence, unity.

If the extremes—pure unity and pure variety—are inconceivable, then the world is in part unitary and in part various. Insofar, it exhibits beauty. This does not mean that the world and everything therein is ideally beautiful, but only that failure to achieve harmonious, vivid feelings is in each case relative rather than absolute.[28] A whole series of values is theoretically possible, "beginning at zero and going toward either an open or

---

28. See Hartshorne, "Structure of Metaphysics," p. 237.

a closed infinity, that is, toward a definite maximum, or simply toward more and more with no possibility of an absolute limit." [29] The higher the value, the greater the unity as well as the variety, each value representing a balance of the two. That unity and variety can increase concomitantly is, once more, due to the multidimensionality of existence.

Materialism and mind-matter dualism each violate the aesthetic criterion but in different respects. Materialism has but one principle, and thus it offers nothing by way of contrast at the categorial level. Dualism offers an absolute contrast, its two principles being left without any hint of connection. We may regard materialism as a monstrosity, a unity without balance by diversity, and dualism as its mirror image, a diversity without balance by unity. At the same time, however, we may adopt another perspective. Thus, we may take the materialist's description extensionally and turn attention to the items of dead matter which he claims are the sole ingredients of reality. Each is external to all the others. Hence, there are no *real* relations, no concrete bonds, in the materialist's world. This chunk of matter is to the right of that one, the motion of this atom succeeds the motion of that one, this planet circles that sun, etc. But none of these relations makes the least bit of difference to the entities involved. Each is fully itself independently of such relations, which are therefore only relations in idea,

29. Hartshorne. *Man's Vision of God*, p. 213.

that is, logical relations. Of course, it is difficult to see what ideas (and hence relations in idea) can mean on the materialist hypothesis, since there are no minds to have them. Where real relations are lacking, there is obviously no participation: things are in no sense members one of another. And with participation goes interest, concern, enjoyment, love, suffering, and knowledge—unless these are wholly self-directed. But still, how can anything relate to itself if it has no feeling or memory, no emotion or desire? It cannot. Materialism therefore entails total extrusion of value or quality from reality. We are left with a sheer multiplicity of "vacuous actualities" (Whitehead), void of all psychical attributes. From this perspective, then, materialism is pluralism with a vengeance, or, in the terms of our aesthetic criterion, diversity bereft of unity.

Classical atomism is one basic form of materialistic pluralism, a triumph of external relations, each atom being conceived as without connection to any other and completely disparate from the surrounding space. We can make sense of external relations if—but only if—there are individual things of which and to which the relations are external. But what is it that gives a classical atom or any other purely material entity its individuality? Such entities seem to be pluralities rather than unities. For why is one part of the entity "with" another part of the same entity any more than it is "with" parts of a second entity? Why, in other words, do the parts belong to "the same entity"? Perhaps it will be said tnat a material entity is a unity because surrounded by empty space. If so, however, two entities touching each other (that is, having no space separating them) would have to be taken as one! The problem of individuation can, of course, be transferred from the entity to its parts. For why is any part *a* part at all? Will we be told that material entities, like the medieval deity, are each simple and without parts—or (more likely) that this is true of their parts, their "atoms"? Surely the idea of a unity without parts has been exposed as nonsense by modern criticism of classical theology. Moreover, the retreat to pure simplicity, whether in the case of God or the atom, leaves the world itself without unity. Why is it a cosmos instead of a chaos?

Simply to add mind to an otherwise materialistic picture of the world is scarcely to solve the problem of unity. For in addition to the question as to how, given a strict materialism, there can be any unity, there is also the question as to how, if a dualism is introduced, matter or quantity is to be unified with mind or quality. Hartshorne remarks that "in experience this unity is the unity of experience as such, and as essentially social, that is, at once relational [structural or quantitative] and with private qualitative characters by virtue of which relations have terms." [30] So if dualism adds the categorial contrast of which materialism deprives us, it fails to give coherence to that contrast, a coherence which can only

----

30. Ibid., p. 217.

be accounted for by "experience as such, and as essentially social." Moreover, the coherence of the world, of which we are also deprived by materialism, is explained by experience as well—that is, if experience is taken to include a theistic form. Thereby, the unity-in-contrast of God and creatures, absent in materialism and dualism alike, is secured. In sum, materialism, lacking any principle by which to furnish the world with concrete bonds, and lacking as well a variety of categorial levels, is essentially inaesthetic. And dualism is no real improvement.

And how does determinism fare when measured by the aesthetic criterion? Determinism asserts in effect that novelty is an illusion due to our limited knowledge of causes. Thus, there is really nothing new under the sun—or anywhere else. If we but knew, the world would be unspeakably boring! Part of the zest and excitement of the present concerns surprises the future will bring. The point is axiomatic in the arts. And skillful artists learn to combine the expected with the surprising— theme with variation, rhythm with innovation, etc. So the future that comes contrasts, if ever so slightly, with that which was anticipated. Otherwise, the relationship of present to future is monotonous, devitalized by lack of contrast.[31] "Even in looking at a picture we have surprises; for we do not grasp the picture all at once, and as we concentrate on one portion we are only partially

31. See Hartshorne, *Reality as Social Process*, p. 50.

prepared for what closer scrutiny of the other portions will reveal." [32] But the merging of the old with the new is also illustrated outside the arts, the unexpected spicing the uniform and regular, and bringing aesthetic satisfaction. Science, to take Hartshorne's example, is constantly attended by surprise and discovery, which are vital to its value.[33] We could almost say, Hartshorne comments, that science predicts everything better than its own future.[34] Of course, contemporary science does not pretend to predict any future state of affairs with certainty or in detail. Nature avoids monotony by employing contrast even in its structures, for example, in wave phenomena or in the "complementarity" of the wave packet. Again, there is the remarkable quantum shift, an electron jumping from one energy level to another and thus achieving a sharp contrast between its two states.[35] Even the laws of nature may be changing, slowly and (to us) imperceptibly, so that the notion of immutable physical laws is as groundless as that of "fixed species." There is but a single immutable principle in nature or life, namely, process or change—unless, of course, determinism be true.

There can be no doubt that determinism represents the world as ugly and dull in the extreme. With each entity entailing all the others, there is absolutely no

32. Ibid., p. 51.
33. See ibid., p. 49.
34. See ibid.
35. See ibid., pp. 47–48.

place for contrast. Indeed, it seems that we have returned to the doctrine of unity without variety, applied in this case to reality as a whole. To one who had "the eyes to see," there would be neither surprise nor even expectation, only the weary spectacle of all in all. For were the future to add even the least item, that item would be externally related to its causes, hence, not determined by them, hence, not predictable from them. The implication, as we said previously, is simply that on the determinist platform futurity—indeed, time itself—is illusory. But as the adage says, familiarity breeds contempt. Can anything be more aesthetically contemptible than the 'unrelieved familiarity of an eternally stagnant world? How fortunate that mere mortals are safe from such exalted perspectives!

The problem of unity without variety has plagued theism no less than atheism. We have already mentioned that classical theologians insisted on the sheer simplicity of God. Perhaps the doctrine of the Trinity should be viewed as their means of mitigating not only the absurdity but the horror of an absolute lack of parts and inner complexity. But "what is required is maximal contrast, not only on one level, as between persons of the Trinity, but between levels within the unity of God—for instance, between the contingent or changing and the necessary or immutable." [36] With respect to the two levels mentioned, theists have tended to divide

36. Hartshorne, *Man's Vision of God*, p. 218.

in either-or fashion. Some have claimed that God is the *ens necessarium*, without "shadow of turning," others that he is personally and dramatically involved in "mighty acts"—though theoretically the drama could include even his death. The latter point of view, empirical theism, has affinity with its counterpart, empirical atheism, for both exclude divine necessity. Only in dipolar theism do we get both contingency and necessity in harmony. God as strictly necessary is in absolute contrast with the world, so that "reality, as composed of God and the world, was [in traditional theology] ugly by defect of unity." [37] Yet, if—as in empirical views, whether theistic or atheistic—God and the world are not distinguished in modality but are each contingent, then reality, as composed of God and world, suffers by defect of contrast.

Let the unity of God be conceived as the unity of reality itself, and the result will be maximal diversity within that unity. For not only will God in this conception embrace all the variety of the creatures, but he will as the principle of coherence in reality contrast categorially with creaturely contingency. By what power can God unify the world's diversity? By the power of his matchless passivity—by the power of "the divine relativity," to use the title of one of Hartshorne's works. Far from being impassive, as in classical thought, "God is the mirror of countless finite individuals, endlessly varying

---

37. Ibid., p. 219.

the theme of personality, whose range of variations only his uniquely sympathetic, flexible personality can span." [38] Atheism is powerless to account for the unity of things, and in the final analysis it leaves the world a hideous pluralism. To be sure, the harmony of all things in God will not be free of discord, hatred, and suffering.[39] For creatures each enjoy a measure of freedom; God's art is not to manipulate automata but to set optimal limits in terms of which the creatures may exercise their freedom. The cosmic play, as Hartshorne says, is not without tragic aspects, for the playwright as well as for the players.[40] Nonetheless, the cosmic art, which is the life of God, is "sublime in its infinite past and present, sublime in its potencies for the future, sublime in the contrast between these, sublime in its multiplicity and variety of parts, sublime in the wholeness to which their partiality is relative."[41]

---

38. Ibid., p. 221.
39. See ibid., p. 227.
40. See ibid.
41. Ibid., p. 226.

>>>>>>>>>>>>>>>>>>>>>>>>>>>>> **8**

A CRITICAL LOOK AT
CRUCIAL AXIOMS

《《《《《《《《《《《《《《《《《《《《《《《《

ONE OF THE WAYS BY WHICH TO EVALUATE A PHILO-
sophical system is to examine its axioms. They are the
foundations, often hidden from view, on which the
system rests. It can be no stronger than they are. What
are the axioms of Hartshorne's metaphysics? Some of
them have already been brought to light in previous
chapters. We wish to put them forth again here, this
time as part of a body of basic assumptions in terms of
which Hartshorne's thought is to be judged.

To begin with, Hartshorne is a rationalist. It is axiomatic for him that reason is to be trusted: "About the
age of seventeen, after reading Emerson's *Essays*, I
made up my mind (doubtless with a somewhat hazy
notion of what I was doing) to trust reason to the end." [1]
His trust in reason has not meant scorn for empiricism,
nor indifference toward it. According to Hartshorne, the
attempt to assay the truth of ideas takes two main forms,

---

1. Hartshorne, *The Logic of Perfection*, p. viii.

one empirical, the other metaphysical.[2] Both are rational in the general sense of the term, and both express the basic faith that discovery of truth is possible as well as worthwhile. But the metaphysician, unlike the empiricist, attempts to abstract from all that is special in order to describe the categories applicable to all possible worlds. This calls for a nonempirical method. That method has often been misconceived. Metaphysics does not begin with truths that are seen to be indubitable and from these deduce implications that are equally clear and certain. Self-evidence is the goal of the inquiry, sought by bringing out the meaning of tentative descriptions of the metaphysically ultimate.[3]

Hartshorne's rationalism has not imprisoned him within the confines of a stodgy dialectic. In all his works he exhibits skill in argumentation, particularly in his brilliant defense of the ontological argument, where close-knit logic is used to great effect. Yet reasoning is matched with originality and insight. As he ranges widely over philosophical topics, Hartshorne brings a freshness and independence of mind, often illuminating as well as persuading his reader. We have already indicated that for him reason is no enemy of faith, rationalism itself being an expression of faith or trust. "What needs justification is not faith in general, for to think, as to live, is already to accept faith as valid."[4] Rather,

2. See Hartshorne, *Reality as Social Process*, p. 163.
3. See ibid., p. 175.
4. Ibid., p. 164.

it is particular faiths—that is, verbal, institutional, ritualistic, and artistic forms of general faith—that must be justified. Reason counsels forbearance in comparing and assessing diverse faiths; it calls for a technical suspension of personal preference in favor of a careful weighing of evidence and argument. Of course, rational neutrality is an ideal seldom if ever fully realized in practice. And even if it were practiced, it would not finally and conclusively decide that some given faith is the true one. Yet reason is not unavailing, and at the metaphysical level, it is quite indispensable. When we are dealing with the concrete or personal, reason must defer to faith. But as we move toward the universal and abstract, reason becomes more and more germane and in metaphysics finds its supreme opportunity. Hartshorne has demonstrated how reason can take advantage of this opportunity.

A second Hartshornian axiom, one to which we have already referred, is that to be (or to be true or false) is to be capable of being known somehow.[5] Thus, what can be known to no being at all simply cannot be, and statements allegedly about unknowable things are really gibberish. To say that everything is capable of being known *somehow* is to suggest that some things may be incapable of being known in all ways or to all knowers. We are aware that what is really possible may not be technically feasible, and that what is logically conceiv-

---

5. See Unpublished Manuscript, p. 17.

able may not be really possible. But, according to Hartshorne, nothing that is can transcend the possibility of
being known in some way by some knower, at least in
principle. It may be that a thing can be known in one
way but not in another. For example, a simple quality
can only be felt. "There is nothing in it to think, if by
thought is meant relating; for a simple quality is not
a relationship." [6] Furthermore, it may be that only God
can know certain entities or know whether such and
such is the case. But of all things and of all truths,
knowledge of some sort, divine or creaturely, must be
possible.

As we have seen, Hartshorne uses this axiom for
methodological purposes. It supports his contention that
"no world at all" is an impossibility. This, of course, is
an instance of a more general usage. For the axiom is
used to show that the denial of *any* metaphysical principle is nonsensical, since the denial, being a sheer negation, could not be known to be true. Also, Hartshorne
argues by way of the axiom that the past must be preserved in God's memory: it must everlastingly be true
that things, having been, will always have been just as
they were, but to none save God, the omniscient knower,
could the past be known in all its immensity and detail.

The contention that being-capable-of-being-known-
somehow is essential to the reality or truth of a thing
entails the thesis that all mystery is provisional, all pri-

---

6. Hartshorne, *Man's Vision of God*, p. 223.

vacy conditional. But why should there not be inaccessible realities, or truths beyond finding out? Why should there not be depths that cannot be plumbed? In taking his stand on this issue, Hartshorne reveals his affinity for the idealist tradition. Still, he holds the realist doctrine that an occurrence is externally related to any subsequent occurrence which has it as object. The explanation he gives is that while "relation to a particular subject knowing an entity is extrinsic to that entity . . . relation to subjectivity in general is not thus extrinsic." [7] But this does not answer the question as to why the entity should require some subject or other (none in particular) to make it an object. Moreover, might there not be aspects or features of the entity which could not be known? One might argue that since an entity as occurring is unknown (the entity being external to the entities in its past as well as to those contemporary with it), its existence can hardly depend on its knowability. For if, though unknown, it exists, why must the potentiality of its being known be necessary to its existence? The argument, however, is not cogent. Nonactualization of a potentiality does not imply the absence or the contingency of the potentiality itself. The argument aside, our question remains: need an entity (or a truth) be knowable? Hartshorne says that the independence of a thing from possible knowledge of it is to him violently counterintuitive.[8] To those who do not share his intui-

_____

7. Hartshorne, *Reality as Social Process*, p. 71.
8. See Unpublished Manuscript, p. 17.

tion, Hartshorne's axiom will seem arbitrary, and it will carry little or no conviction. The acceptance or rejection of the axiom may in the final analysis remain a matter of intuition.

Another of Hartshorne's axioms, closely related to the one just discussed, is that the known is contained in the knower. As we have seen, the known is not just represented to the knower by sensations or ideas—that is, if by knowing we mean concrete awareness. Creaturely knowing is, of course, deficient in the appropriation of the known, only divine knowledge being fully adequate to its objects. Thus, only God includes what he knows without distortion and without remainder. In principle, however, relation to X includes X. If the world is a great "ocean of feelings," then knowledge of the world is knowledge of feeling, not just of abstractions from feeling. But—to refer to a point made above—one cannot "think" a quality or feeling. In order to know it, one must possess it as a factor of feeling within his own experience. Furthermore, if something known were not included in the knowledge of it, the truth would insofar escape the knower. How then would the something be known? Perhaps by inference. But the concrete cannot be inferred from the abstract. Moreover, anything inferred is thereby possessed. If not, can the inferred be anything known?

The axiom under discussion is, of course, fundamental to Hartshorne's metaphysics. It underlies his doctrine of social relatedness, of causality, of time, and of

God. An object is something felt by a subject. In being felt the object becomes a constituent and hence a cause of the subject. The subject appropriates the object-cause (along with others) in its own novel synthesis, and this "creative advance" (Whitehead) constitutes the passage from past to present. God is, of course, the subject (or subject-sequence) to whom no object-cause is strange, the individual whose inexhaustible receptivity guarantees the inevitability of his existence.

Thus, time is enrichment, addition—not loss or destruction. To some, *this* may seem counterintuitive, especially when time is interpreted in terms of the object-to-subject relation. If a mouse glances my way, is he then my superior, the knower including the known?[9] Or if I experience God, am I, on the same principle, his superior? Hartshorne argues that there is a difference between the mere experience of something and what might be called the effective experience of it, full consciousness being the criterion of effectiveness here.[10] Obviously, we are not fully conscious of many of the influences upon us, yet they are not simply unexperienced by us. So too the mouse, though he is aware of me, is far from fully conscious of me and therefore he includes me only in a vague sense. My inclusion of God is even vaguer—perhaps infinitely so—though I do experience him in some inadequate way.

Surely the most ticklish point here is how to make

9. See Hartshorne, "The Structure of Givenness," p. 33.
10. See ibid., pp. 33–34.

sense of the idea that an occurrence now past is yet a constituent of a present knower, even if the knower is God himself. The problem is not that the past occurrence would be indistinguishable from its present knower, for the former is to be conceived as part of the latter. The problem is rather that the full particularity of the past occurrence seems unavailable to any knower. Hartshorne is, of course, aware of this objection, and he undertakes to answer it.[11] In doing so, he employs Whitehead's distinction between subjective and objective forms of feeling: a past occurrence is in itself a subject, but as known it is an object. Thus, to use Hartshorne's example, "I feel *how* the other felt, I do not feel *as* the other felt." [12] Nor does God feel *as* the other felt. For instance, if we have placed confidence in a fallacious hypothesis, the omniscient being, though he knows we have done so, does not follow suit. "God feels how we trust the hypothesis, but he does not trust it."[13] Very well, but what about our very trust itself? Is it known and preserved? Or put more generally, is the occurring of an event known and preserved? This appears impossible, for an event can be known only if it has already occurred. Then and only then is it a datum. Yet, if events as occurring cannot be known, Hartshorne's second axiom will have to be

---

11. See ibid., pp. 33 ff.; see also "Comment by Professor Charles Hartshorne," in Eugene H. Peters, *The Creative Advance* (St. Louis: Bethany Press, 1966), pp. 140–43.

12. Hartshorne, "The Structure of Givenness," p. 33.

13. Ibid., p. 35.

severely qualified. For then something is unknowable—
unless, of course, occurring is itself nothing. But surely
occurring is not nothing. If it were, there could be no
subject that was not an object for some actual subject
subsequent to it. That is, there would only be events-
having-occurred, but no events-occurring.

Sticking with the distinction between subjective and
objective forms of feeling, we can explain how God
knows all things, including ignorance, false belief, and
moral evil, without having them as they are in themselves but only as they are as objects. The absurdity of
God's sharing creaturely faults and frailties is thus
avoided. But how then can time be sheer addition? Something of the past is missing even from the most exalted
knowledge of it. Otherwise, to take the example above,
God would actually trust the fallacious hypothesis. That
trust is missing in him, though, of course, he knows *of* it.
This means that there is loss in temporal passage, not
just gain. Hartshorne, we know, repudiates the idea of
temporal loss and insists that God is absolutely all-
inclusive. We cannot have it both ways, however. Either
there is or there is not loss, and the difficulties in main-
taining the latter option seem formidable.

The axiom that the knower (ideally) includes the
known is connected with still another axiom, that the
actual is the definite, the possible the indefinite.[14] For

---

14. See Hartshorne, *Man's Vision of God*, p. 225; his
Reality as Social Process, pp. 88, 94, 96, 98, and 99; and Unpublished Manuscript, p. 77.

if actuality X "conforms to the law of excluded middle as applied to predicates," [15] what in X could possibly be opaque to a sufficiently penetrating knower? Of course, actualities transcend the grasp of reason, which operates instead with universals. But to the definite must correspond definite truth, to be possessed intuitively.[16]

Now, there is little reason to doubt that the actual is definite, but is definiteness the very meaning of actuality? To the question, *What* is it that is definite? we might very well answer: the event, the actuality itself, is definite. This answer suggests an instance-property distinction, a distinction which Hartshorne, of course, respects.[17] The event or actuality "has" definiteness, as we sometimes put it, but can we say that it is itself definiteness? And if not, how shall we conceive it? The interpretation of actuality is surely a major responsibility of any metaphysics. The actual must somehow be distinguished from the merely possible. According to Hartshorne, actualization involves the shutting out of alternative possibilities, a process by which the possibilities are restricted to the proximate potentiality of some particular P. But, says Hartshorne, none of the alternatives within that potentiality coincides with P, which when it occurs will possess additional definiteness—a sheer

---

15. Hartshorne, *Reality as Social Process*, p. 88; see his "Structure of Metaphysics," p. 230.

16. See Unpublished Manuscript, p. 77.

17. See Hartshorne, *The Logic of Perfection*, p. 66.

creation.[18] Obviously, no matter how far possibility is restricted, what remains is nonetheless possibility, so that creation is required if the actual is to be distinguished from the possible. The question is whether that creation is adequately conceived as new definiteness. Some philosophers have argued that actuality must differ in principle, not just in degree, from possibility. Indeed, if the difference is strictly one of degree (of definiteness), it seems that restriction of possibility, carried far enough, will yield the actual. After all, new definiteness always results whenever (and however) old indefiniteness is restricted.

Hartshorne's axiom of positivity is implicit in his theory of actuality as limitation or restriction of possibility. For a negative fact is simply a possible state of affairs condemned to nonactualization by the realization of some alternative state. Negative fact means excluded fact, the exclusion being effected by the included, positive fact. One may wonder whether this doctrine—which may very well be applicable in most cases—need be universally true. If so, the consequences for metaphysics are immense, as Hartshorne observes.[19] But is the axiom of positivity "a mere truism"?[20] Those who believe there might have been (or may be) nothing at all would, of course, argue that negativity need not

18. See Hartshorne, *Reality as Social Process*, p. 98.
19. See Hartshorne, "Negative Facts and the Analogical Inference to 'Other Mind,' " p. 151.
20. See ibid., p. 152.

involve exclusion by positive fact. For were nothing existent, nothing would be actualized and therefore nothing excluded. To point to the paradoxes of "nothing at all" does not, however, confirm Hartshorne's axiom (if indeed an axiom can be confirmed). The axiom seems really to gain its force from the second axiom and perhaps should be considered a corollary of that axiom— that to be (or be true) is to be capable of being known. A purely negative fact would be unknowable, unless it was known to deity, and there seems to be no clear explanation as to how even he might know it. The axiom of positivity, of course, has intuitive and perhaps even common-sense support. For why should not some perfectly possible state of affairs obtain in place of the one that does obtain? Does it just "happen" to be un-realized? We naturally appeal to experience to shed light on the question. We know that we must renounce one possibility in order to realize another, in short, that "we can't have our cake and eat it too." But now we have returned to the doctrine of factual exclusiveness and hence to the axiom of positivity.

The axiom suggests the inseparability of the possible and the actual, and in turn the inseparability of the cate-gorial contrasts. We are thus in sight of another of Harts-horne's axioms, the axiom of polarity. In the last two chapters we became well acquainted with this axiom. Its importance in Hartshorne's system can hardly be overestimated. It is the basis of "the Hartshornian econ-omy" and the principle upon which turns his reinterpretation of the ontological argument. The divine dipolarity is one very important application of the general doctrine of polar contrast. God's existence is the necessary, abstract law of his being; his actuality is the contingent, concrete states of his experience. The law is merely that there *be* some such state.

A categorial contrast may be considered either intensionally or extensionally. Taken intensionally, a pair of ultimate contraries is a pair of logically interdependent concepts. Either of them entails the other. Taken extensionally, the pair represents two logically different levels of reality. The one is concrete, the other abstract, the relation between the two being asymmetrical. That Hartshorne has conceived the poles (extensionally) in the asymmetry of whole and part is surely testimony to his genius. The conception enables him to explain the unity of contrasting dimensions of reality, dimensions which philosophers have often compared invidiously or simply treated dualistically.

Whatever difficulties Hartshorne's "higher synthesis" may involve, his doctrine of categorial contrast remains one of the most masterful of metaphysical theories. That theory unites the ideal of coherence and the ideal of harmony in a single principle. For the contrasting categories are seen to belong together not just conceptually but aesthetically as well. For they exhibit the fundamental aesthetic principle of diversity within unity. Reality, on this interpretation, accords with the mind's deliberations, as with the heart's aspirations.

The future of this interpretation and indeed of neo-classical metaphysics depends in large measure on how Hartshorne's six crucial axioms fare among philosophers. In this chapter we have suggested some of the difficulties which those axioms involve. Perhaps none of the difficulties mentioned constitutes what Hartshorne's teacher Rufus Jones called an impasse—which Jones insisted every system contains. Further critical work is needed. There has, in fact, been a dearth of careful criticism of Hartshorne's writings, as he himself points out. One of the reasons his writings have not received the attention they deserve is that in Anglo-American philosophy metaphysics has been in eclipse. There are at present indications that this eclipse is about over. One of the indications is that Hartshorne, now at the height of a career stretching back more than forty years, is coming into a position of genuine prominence in American philosophy. He has for decades been influential among American theologians, and his influence with them is stronger today than ever before.

Hartshorne is not to be viewed as a mere exception or sport in modern philosophy. While antimetaphysical philosophy has gained strength, particularly in the twentieth century, metaphysics has been championed by an impressive line of philosophers, many of them men of high rank and distinction. "While the opponents of metaphysics have been somewhat noisily sharpening their critical weapons, metaphysicians have been quietly improving their constructive doctrines." [21] Since the middle of the nineteenth century the metaphysical stream has been enriched by the thought of Fechner, Peirce, James, Royce, Bergson, Hocking, Alexander, Whitehead, Varisco, Aliotta, Scheler, Ward, Boutroux, Lequier, Montague, Parker, Garnett, Boodin, Tillich, Weiss, Blanshard, and others.[22] Among these thinkers there has been a certain rough agreement, a partial convergence in philosophical outlook. Hartshorne stands in this distinguished tradition. He is closest to Peirce and Whitehead, but has followed neither slavishly. Today many are in Hartshorne's debt for his courageous and far-reaching explorations in speculative philosophy. He is to many of us the foremost of contemporary philosophers.

21. Unpublished Manuscript, p. 1.
22. See Hartshorne, *Reality as Social Process*, p. 131.

BIBLIOGRAPHY

«««««««««««««««««««««

Chapter 1: Charles Hartshorne

The reader may wish to examine Hartshorne's somewhat autobiographical reflections in his Preface to *Reality as Social Process: Studies in Metaphysics and Religion* (Glencoe, Ill.: Free Press, 1953), as well as those in his Comment at the end of Eugene H. Peters, *The Creative Advance* (St. Louis: Bethany Press, 1966).

Chapter 2: The Methodological Key

Hartshorne's works with special importance for the discussion in this chapter include: *Beyond Humanism: Essays in the Philosophy of Nature* (Chicago: Willett, Clark and Company, 1937); reissued in paperback as a Bison Book by the University of Nebraska Press (Lincoln, 1968). Chapter 16, "Logical Positivism and the Method of Philosophy," presents some of Hartshorne's early methodological reflections. In his *Reality as Social Process: Studies in Metaphysics and Religion* (Glencoe, Ill.: Free Press, 1953), chapter 10, "Two Levels of Faith and Reason," contains relevant material. Hartshorne's and William L. Reese's *Philosophers Speak of God* (Chicago: University of Chicago Press, 1953) has many passages which bear upon metaphysical method; important among these is the introductory essay, "The Standpoint of Panentheism." In his *The Logic of Perfection and Other Essays in Neoclassical Metaphysics* (La Salle, Ill.: Open Court Publishing Company,

1962), see especially chapter 12, "Some Empty Though Important Truths." Hartshorne's forthcoming book, *Creative Synthesis and Philosophic Method* (London: SCM Press), to be published in 1970 and distributed in the United States by Open Court, will incorporate the content of his Unpublished Manuscript (cited herein). The book will represent his most significant discussion of metaphysical method.

Hartshorne has devoted a number of articles to the discussion of metaphysical method, among them the following: "Strict and Genetic Identity: An Illustration of the Relations of Logic to Metaphysics," in *Structure, Method, and Meaning: Essays in Honor of Henry M. Sheffer* (New York: Liberal Arts Press, 1951); "Metaphysical Statements as Nonrestrictive and Existential," *The Review of Metaphysics* 12, no. 1 (September 1958): 35–47; "The Structure of Metaphysics: A Criticism of Lazerowitz's Theory," *Philosophy and Phenomenological Research* 19, no. 2 (December 1958): 226–40; "Metaphysics and the Modality of Existential Judgments," in *The Relevance of Whitehead*, ed. Ivor Leclerc (New York: Macmillan Company, 1961); "Real Possibility," *The Journal of Philosophy* 60, no. 21 (October 1963): 593–605; "Negative Facts and the Analogical Inference to 'Other Mind,'" no. 21 in *Dr. S. Radhakrishnan Souvenir Volume*, ed. J. P. Atreya et al. (Moradabad, India: Darshana International, 1964), pp. 147–52; and "What Metaphysics Is," *The Journal of Karnatak University—Social Sciences* (Dharwar, India): 3 (1967): 1–15.

Chapter 3: Panpsychism

Three previously cited Hartshorne works are recommended for study with this chapter: *Beyond Humanism: Essays in the Philosophy of Nature*, in which the reader should see chapter 11, "Mind and Matter," and chapter 12, "Mind and Body: Organic Sympathy"; *Reality as Social Process: Studies in Metaphysics and Religion*, the first four chapters of which are especially relevant; and *The Logic of Perfection and Other Essays in Neoclassical Metaphysics*, in which discussions of panpsychism will be found in chapter 7, "A World of Organisms," chapter 8, "Mind, Matter, and Freedom," and chapter 13, "The Unity of Man and the Unity of Nature."

Also recommended are the following articles by Hartshorne: "Panpsychism," in *A History of Philosophical Systems*, ed. Vergilius Ferm (Ames, Iowa: Littlefield, Adams and Co., 1958); "Interrogation of Charles Hartshorne (conducted by William Alston)," in *Philosophical Interrogations*, ed. Sydney and Beatrice Rome (New York: Holt, Rinehart and Winston, 1964), particularly Section II, "Feeling" (pp. 331–37); and "Psychology and the Unity of Knowledge," *The Southern Journal of Philosophy* 5, no. 2 (Summer 1967): 81–90.

Chapter 4: Determinism and the Creationist View of Time

Hartshorne's *Beyond Humanism: Essays in the Philosophy of Nature*, already cited, is also useful in respect to this topic; see particularly chapter 10, "Indeterminism in Psychology and Ethics." One of Hartshorne's finest statements of his doctrine of creativity is chapter 5, "Chance, Love, and Incompatibility," in *Reality as Social Process: Studies in Metaphysics and Religion*, also already cited. Of special interest in the earlier mentioned *The Logic of Perfection and Other Essays in Neoclassical Metaphysics* are chapter 6, "Freedom Requires Indeterminism and Universal Causality," and chapter 8, "Mind, Matter, and Freedom."

One of Hartshorne's early contributions to the topic, one of special merit, is his "Contingency and the New Era in Metaphysics (I)," *The Journal of Philosophy* 29, no. 16 (August 1932): 421–31, part II of which appears in the subsequent issue of *The Journal of Philosophy* [29, no. 17 (August 1932): 457–69] and completes the essay. Other discussions include Hartshorne's "Causal Necessities: An Alternative to Hume," *The Philosophical Review* 63, no. 4 (October 1954): 479–99; his "The Philosophy of Creative Synthesis," *The Journal of Philosophy* 55, no. 22 (October 1958): 944–53; and his "The

Idea of Creativity in American Philosophy," *The Journal of Karnatak University—Social Sciences* (Dharwar, India) 2 (1966): 1—13.

Chapter 5: Neoclassical Theism

Hartshorne has written extensively in this area. The following books, listed in chronological order of publication, are among his basic contributions on neoclassical theism: the previously cited *Beyond Humanism: Essays in the Philosophy of Nature; Man's Vision of God and the Logic of Theism* (Chicago: Willett, Clark and Company, 1941), reissued by Archon Books (Hamden, Conn., 1964); *The Divine Relativity: A Social Conception of God* (New Haven: Yale University Press, 1948); two forenamed books, *Reality as Social Process: Studies in Metaphysics and Religion,* and Hartshorne's and Reese's *Philosophers Speak of God;* the previously cited *The Logic of Perfection and Other Essays in Neoclassical Metaphysics,* where he develops the neoclassical form of the ontological argument in chapter 2, "Ten Ontological or Modal Proofs for God's Existence"; *Anselm's Discovery: A Re-examination of the Ontological Proof for God's Existence* (La Salle, Ill.: Open Court Publishing Company, 1965); and *A Natural Theology for Our Time* (La Salle, Ill.: Open Court Publishing Company, 1967).

Hartshorne's articles on theism in journals and books are so numerous that a brief list is quite inexhaustive. The following, however, are among his important contributions in this area: "The Formal Validity and Real Significance of the Ontological Argument," *The Philosophical Review* 53, no. 3 (May 1944): 225—45; "Tillich's Doctrine of God," in *The Theology of Paul Tillich,* ed. Charles W. Kegley and Robert W. Bretall (New York: Macmillan Company, 1952); "The Idea of God—Literal or Analogical?" *The Christian Scholar* 39, no. 2 (June 1956): 131—36; "Introduction to the Second Edition," *St. Anselm: Basic Writings,* trans. S. N. Deane (La Salle, Ill.: Open Court Publishing Company, 1962);

"What Did Anselm Discover?" *Union Seminary Quarterly Review* 17, no. 3 (March 1962): 213–22 (included in an expanded version as chapter 17 of *The Many-faced Argument,* ed. John H. Hick and Arthur C. McGill [New York: Macmillan Company, 1967]; Section IV, "God" (pp. 342–47), of "Interrogation of Charles Hartshorne (conducted by William Alston)," in *Philosophical Interrogations,* ed. Sydney and Beatrice Rome (New York: Holt, Rinehart and Winston, 1964); and "The Dipolar Conception of Deity," *The Review of Metaphysics* 21, no. 2 (December 1967): 273–89.

Chapter 6: The Hartshornian Economy

Among Hartshorne's writings which bear upon this discussion are his "Strict and Genetic Identity: An Illustration of the Relations of Logic to Metaphysics," in the aforementioned *Structure, Method, and Meaning: Essays in Honor of Henry M. Sheffer;* his "Chance, Love, and Incompatibility," in the previously cited *Reality as Social Process: Studies in Metaphysics and Religion;* his Introduction, "The Standpoint of Panentheism," in his and Reese's *Philosophers Speak of God,* cited above; his "The Structure of Givenness," *The Philosophical Forum* 18 (1960–61): 22–39; and his "What Metaphysics Is," *The Journal of Karnatak University—Social Sciences* (Dharwar, India) 3 (1967): 1–15.

Chapter 7: The Aesthetic Motif

One of Hartshorne's early but very valuable discussions of aesthetics is chapter 5, "Dualism in Aesthetics," in *The Philosophy and Psychology of Sensation* (Chicago: University of Chicago Press, 1934); the whole of this book which, unfortunately, is out of print, concerns the aesthetic motif. Two of his works cited in connection with earlier chapters also pertain here: *Man's Vision of God and the Logic of Theism,* especially chapter 6, "God and the Beautiful"; and *Reality as Social Process: Studies in Metaphysics and Religion,* in which chapter 2, "Harmony in Life and Nature," is especially relevant.

Hartshorne's "Sense Quality and Feeling Tone," *Proceedings of the Seventh International Congress of Philosophy,* ed. Gilbert Ryle (Oxford: Oxford University Press, 1931), is an early contribution but an important one. For a recent discussion, see Hartshorne's "The Aesthetics of Birdsong," *The Journal of Aesthetics and Art Criticism* 26, no. 3 (Spring 1968) : 311–15.

INDEX

Existential statement(s), 20, 24

Experience, 96, 99–100, 102; as principle of individuality, 33; flexibility of, 34; and extendedness, 35–36, 38, 88; as relational, 81–82, 84; as gain in definiteness, 85; and unity, 105–6; mere, and effective, 117

Extended, the, 77

Extendedness, 35–37

Extension, 38–40, 77, 88

Fact(s), 17–19, 21–22, 24–26

Facticity, 17–18

Factuality, 25–26

Faith, 112–13

Fallacy of Misplaced Concreteness, 38

Falsifiability, 23, 28

Falsification, 19

Fechner Gustav Theodor, 125

Feeling(s), 14, 16, 33, 35, 84; social structure of, 39, 41, 98; sensation as, 95, 99–100; cannot think, 116; subjective and objective forms of, 118–19

Findlay, J. N., 72–73

Freedom, 37, 53–55, 84, 89, 110

Fulbright lecturer, Hartshorne as, 12–13

Galileo, 19

Garnett, Arthur Campbell, 125

German idealism, 5. *See also* Idealism

Giotto, 11

God: and future events, 7, 66; and creatures, 26, 74; influence of, over all, 37; two levels within, 40, 67–70, 90, 108, 123; existence of, 58–59, 65; Anselm's concept of, 61–64, 70–71; as finite, 63; all-inclusiveness of, 63–65, 73, 116, 118–19; as self-surpassing, 64–65; omniscience of, 65, 114, 119; universal relativity of, 66, 70; as personal, 71–72; as orderer of world, 74–75; literally instantiates the categories, 90–91; unity of, 101, 105–6, 108–10; experience of, 117

Goethe University, 12

Gompers, Samuel, 6

Gomperz, Heinrich, 7

Gomperz, Theodor, 7

Great War, 3

Hapgood, Norman, 6

Harmony-in-contrast, 98

Hartmann, Nicolai, 14

Hartshorne, Charles, 1–18, 22–23, 25–27, 35, 38, 40, 42–47, 50–51, 53–59, 62–68, 71–76, 78, 82, 83, 84–98, 100, 105, 107, 110–25

Vacuous actualities, 104. *See also* Dead matter *and* Mere matter
Variety, 101, 103; without unity, 101–2; pure variety, 102
Varisco, Bernardino, 125

Ward, James, 125

Weiss, Paul, 9, 125
Whitehead, Alfred North, 7–10, 14, 38–39, 47, 57, 82, 85, 89, 93, 104, 117–18, 125
Woods, James Haughton, 5–6

Yeates School, 1–2, 4